# BOEING
# B-17
# FLYING FORTRESS

Jane's

# BOEING
# B-17
# FLYING
# FORTRESS

## DAVID C. ISBY

HarperCollins*Publishers*

Harper Collins Publishers
77-85 Fulham Palace Road
Hammersmith,
London, W6 8JB

1  3  5  7  9  10  8  6  4  2

ISBN 0 00 472240 X

Design: Rod Teasdale
Airbrush Artwork: Chris Davey
Computer graphics: Richard Burgess
Photo captions: David Oliver

Copyright 1999, David C. Isby

Dedication: For Lieutenant Colonel Joseph Shackleton,
US Air Force (retired), formerly of the 'Ragged
Irregulars', the 91st Bombardment Group (Heavy), RAF
Bassingbourn; who was there when it mattered most.

# CONTENTS

# INTRODUCTION

**The events in this book are not intended to depict any one B-17 sortie by an actual airplane and crew. Rather it is intended to be a sortie that would have been flown by an Eighth Air Force B-17G as the Bomber Offensive was entering its final and decisive phase, starting after D-Day. No combat mission is typical or routine, so the elements of this one have been selected to be examples of many others.**

*Right; One of the Eighth Air Force's B-17 targets on October 9, 1943 was the Arado works at Ankelm where the Fort's arch enemy, the Focke Wulf Fw 190 was built.*

*Below; A formation of Eighth Air Force Boeing B-17G Flying Fortress bombers of the 381st Bomb Group over Germany approach their target with bomb bay doors open.*

There have been many accounts of the incredible heroism of the aircrew and ruggedness of the aircraft that took part in the Allied Bomber Offensive. This is a composite of them, intended to show not moments of high drama, but what it was like to go to war in the left-hand seat of a B-17G –with sidelong glances at the other nine

men in the crew –and also why it was like that. This means the story of the mission has to start with why the B-17G was designed, and how the units that would take part in the mission were organized. Many of the decisions that will shape this mission's outcome were made a decade before the engine start time.

# THE RISE OF THE B-17

## STRATEGIC BOMBING AND THE USAAF

Ideas produce things. The idea that produced the Boeing B-17 Flying Fortress was strategic bombing, in particular the high-altitude strategic daylight bombing that served as a rationale for the US Army Air Forces (USAAF). These ideas, nurtured in the pre-war years when massed formation of bombers like the B-17 flew only in visionary imaginations, were put to the test on 17 August 1942, when the USAAF entered the strategic bombing campaign over Europe.

industrial base, administrative centers and population's morale –rather than entrenched forces in the field. Air Marshal Hugh 'Boom' Trenchard of the RAF became its main exponent in the interwar years, even though the bombers available in the 1920s were wood and wire biplanes that could take a one-ton bombload just a few hundred miles.

The senior US combat airman of the Great War, Brigadier General William 'Billy' Mitchell, came to believe that airpower, including strategic bombing, would determine

*Right; The US Army Air Corps' only four-engine bomber squadron flies over downtown Manhattan on September 21, 1937. Two years later, when Hitler invaded Poland, there would still only be one four-engine bomber squadron.*

*Above; A close box formation adopted by Eighth Air Force B-17 Fortress groups of six three-ship elements during daylight bombing missions over Germany from 1943-45.*

Strategic bombing had its origins in World War I, in the raids of German Gotha bombers on London and the attacks by the RAF's Independent Force on the Ruhr. Then, the first theoretician of strategic bombing, Italian General Guilio Douhet, saw in the few Caproni biplane bombers –some flown by US crews –dispatched over the Alps the portents of a rapidly improving technology and a way to strike at the enemy without repeating the costly attacks of trench warfare.

The strategic bomber would strike directly at the enemy's will and means to resist –his

the way future wars would be fought. His career ended in inter-service rancor. Following him, at the Air Corps Tactical School - at Maxwell Field, Alabama since 1931 — other airmen started to ask what are perhaps the most important questions anyone can ask in days of peace: what is going to be the nature of the next war? what do we need to do to be able to win it? what does rapid technological change mean for future wars?

The nature of America's next war was uncertain. So bombers with a capability to carry out many types of missions –attacking

inbound invasion convoys was a popular scenario pre-war –would be an advantage. Most serious would be another world war against a major industrial power. To win it, striking directly at the enemy's will and means to resist meant striking at the complex, inter-dependent war economy of a modern state. To do this, they thought at Maxwell, required not wholesale devastation but the elimination of key elements of that economy. This meant building an airplane able to carry large numbers of bombs long distances and deliver them accurately. Which implied having to bomb in daylight. This, in turn, meant that the bomber would have to defeat enemy interceptors through speed, defensive firepower, or both.

In the early 1930s, technology was catching up with theory. Lockheed, Boeing and Douglas produced all-metal, low-wing airliners faster than any of the contemporary biplane fighters. The airliners featured smooth, stressed-skin construction, retractable landing gear, rubber de-icer 'boots' on the leading edge of the wings, underwing flaps (to allow the new low-drag designs the lift they need for landing) and constant speed propellers which changed their blade angle (pitch), and maintained a constant number of revolutions per minute (rpm) regardless of engine speed or load. Since take-off and climb requires low pitch, and cruising high pitch, these new airliners used this to carry loads higher, faster, and longer than any bomber then in service.

The Air Corps –as the USAAF was to be from 1920 until 1940 –could only afford a few new-technology Boeing YB-9 and the Martin B-10 twin engine bombers. What the

men at Maxwell really wanted was a true heavy bomber, such as the Boeing XB-15 and the Douglas XB–of which they ordered single experimental examples. But they knew both technology and funding would be insufficient for large numbers of such flying behemoths. In 1934 the resulting compromise led to a competition for a multi-engine all-metal bomber to replace the B-10.

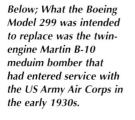

*Below; What the Boeing Model 299 was intended to replace was the twin-engine Martin B-10 meduim bomber that had entered service with the US Army Air Corps in the early 1930s.*

Boeing's entry was a revolutionary four-engine bomber design, the Model 299. Predecessor of the B-17, it incorporated more powerful engines with turbo-superchargers which used a turbine wheel turned by the force of exhaust gasses to compress air and increase the air pressure in the engine manifold, forcing more air inside to improve engine performance. The engines turned Hamilton constant speed propellers. Other technological advances included wing flaps, cowl flaps (to cool the powerful engines), two sets of flight controls (one for a co-pilot), an autopilot, and trim tabs adjustable in flight to help keep the plane straight and level. It ran on 100 octane gasoline, more powerful than any then in use.

The Model 299 crashed on a test flight in 1935 and the competition was won by the mediocre, but cheaper, twin-engine Douglas B-18. However, the airmen had seen the promise in the 299 design, even though it was really a four-engined medium bomber. A squadron of evaluation YB-17s was ordered. The Air Corps, increasingly conscious of living in a pre-war rather than a post-war world, started learning to apply the ideas of airpower to actual bombers and crews.

Ideas need to be translated into things. There were thirteen B-17s in 1939, but by the end of the war some 12,276 had been delivered. In April 1944 production peaked at 16 a day. What made the B-17 available to the USAAF and its strategy was the 'arsenal of democracy': the US war economy and its aircraft industry. Strategic bombing meshed well with the view –associated with US Army Chief of Staff George Marshall –that the main function of the US armed forces was to apply the industrial power of the world's largest economy to the war.

Neither ideas nor things fight modern wars. Institutions do. In its only war, the USAAF proved itself to be a successful military institution, with a remarkable ability to both improve itself and improvise solutions. It remained strong in its chosen primary mission –strategic bombing –while at the same time creating new capabilities ranging from offensive fighter operations to strategic airlift. The steepness of its learning curve, from the tiny formations of 1942 to the massive air armadas of 1944-45 was proof of its fundamental quality. The men with the ideas at Maxwell and the men with the slide rules in the factories at Seattle and San Diego made many mistakes, and there never emerged one common intelligence to guide both doctrine and technology. In the final analysis, however, they got it right.

*Above; A Piper L-4 Grasshopper parked in front of a B-17 gives an idea of the size of the 'giant' four-engine Fortress heavy bomber which had a wingspan of over 103 feet.*

# MISSION BACKGROUND
## THE STRATEGIC BOMBER OFFENSIVE

RAF bombers had been attacking Germany since the day after the declaration of war in 1939. Starting in 1940, they bombed primarily by night, against area targets, after daylight raids suffered heavy losses. In 1941, as US participation in the war against Hitler appeared inevitable, Anglo-American planning talks looked at incorporating the USAAF in the bomber campaign. The USAAF drew up its own plan to do this, AWPD-1, aiming at nothing less than victory through precision strategic daylight bombing of German industry by a massive force of unescorted bombers.

In January 1942, the US Eighth Air Force, was established to implement these plans and moved to England, at first without any combat airplanes. These were frantically being produced, filled with hastily trained crews, and sent across the Atlantic in the summer of 1942. Even before the Eighth's first combat mission, it became apparent that its bombers would need fighter escort to survive, though the numbers and scope of this requirement were greatly underestimated. Groups of Republic P-47 Thunderbolt and Lockheed P-

*Below; B-17s of the 381st Bomb Group on their way to Stuttgart in three-ship elements, on September 5, 1944.*

38 Lightning fighters were soon on their way to England. A newer design, the North American P-51 Mustang, was also promised.

On 17 August 1942, 12 B-17Es bombed the rail yards at Rouen with a heavy escort of RAF Supermarine Spitfires. It proved to be a 'milk run', without strong opposition or losses. Major General Ira Eaker, the Eighth's commander and a firm believer in strategic daylight bombing, led the trail squadron in 'Yankee Doodle'.

For the rest of 1942, as more bomber groups arrived from the United States, the Eighth struck, as weather permitted, at targets throughout occupied western Europe. The training value for crews and staffs alike was considered more valuable than the effect of the bombs dropped. Some groups were sent to Operation Torch, the Allied invasion of northwest Africa and remained in the Mediterranean theater.

The Anglo-American decision not to invade

Europe in 1943, made the bombers the second front. The US resisted British pressure to join in night bombing, and a combined bomber offensive, Operation Pointblank, was planned, using elements of AWPD-1 to guide the US participation.

In January 1943, Wilhelmshaven was the first German city to be hit by the Eighth, using new B-17Fs. In the following months, as more reinforcements arrived from the US, they hit the industrial Ruhr. These missions were beyond the range of the RAF Spitfires and the USAAF P-47 Thunderbolts that flew escort missions, even though the P-47s carried external drop tanks to extend their range. The Germans now, belatedly, realized the power of the US bombers. The bulk of Germany's fighters and flak guns were pulled back from the Mediterranean and eastern fronts and concentrated for the defense of the Reich.

In summer 1943, the Eighth was making deep penetration raids to destroy crucial German industries. But on 17 August, maximum effort strikes on the ball bearing plant at Schweinfurt and the Messerschmitt aircraft plant at Regensburg resulted in the loss of 60 of 360 attacking B-17s. Despite these losses, the offensive continued, striking far beyond the range of fighter escorts, until 14 October, when 290 B-17s again attacked Schweinfurt. Again, 60 B-17s were lost.

No force could sustain losses of such magnitude over a prolonged campaign. Unescorted daylight bombing of Germany was defeated. But as the winter weather closed in, the Eighth Air Force was soon in a position to resume the offensive. New, radar-equipped bombers acted as pathfinders against area targets covered by clouds. A second strategic bombing front was opened by the US Fifteenth Air Force based in Italy's Foggia plain. More aircraft arrived in England, with better trained crews. These included the first new B-17Gs but also new escort fighters. The P-47s and P-38s were soon with multiple, larger drop tanks, extending their reach far into Germany. Most important, the first P-51 Mustangs arrived. With their internal fuel and drop tanks, they could escort the bombers anywhere in Germany.

*Above; A formation of Eighth Air Force Fortress heavy bombers head for a daylight raid on Germany with a fighter escort of P-47s high above them.*

production and forced the German fighter force into battle against the new escort fighters. The German fighter force never recovered. Some 450 German aircraft were lost in the air in those six days alone, probably as many on the ground. US losses totalled 225 bombers and 28 fighters, but it was a casualty rate that could be sustained.

The Eighth belatedly joined in the RAF's offensive against Berlin. In early March 1944, a series of bitterly fought battles saw the Eighth suffer the heaviest bomber losses of the war. However, their escorting P-51s decisively defeated the defending fighters. By 8 March, the Luftwaffe's fighters could no longer rise to challenge an Eighth Air Force maximum effort against their capital.

Hermann Goering said he knew the war was lost when he first saw P-51s unopposed over Berlin. By the end of March, General Spaatz also recognized that, at least, the German day fighter force was defeated. He now saw the opportunity to re-launch the campaign against German industry that the unescorted bombers had attempted the

*Above; A Group of B-17 Fortress bombers form up in three-ship elements over the North Sea as they head for a bombing mission over Germany.*

*Right: At the end of a mission, Crew Chief M/Sgt Penrose Bingaman stencils another bomb on the nose of 'Idiot's Delight', the first B-17F of the 94th Bomb Group to survive 50 missions.*

New commanders came with the new airplanes. Major-General Jimmy Doolittle, who had raided Tokyo in 1942 and made effective use of escorted bombers in the Mediterranean in 1943, took over command of the Eighth Air Force. He was not a Maxwell man –he had not flown a B-17 until a general –but his innovative and active style was evident: both the 100-octane fuel in the B-17's fuel tanks and the 21-ship group formations they flew in were improved by the results of Doolittle's work. Eaker took over the Allied air forces in the Mediterranean. To command both the Eighth and Fifteenth Air Forces, a new headquarters, US Strategic Air Forces Europe, was created under General Carl 'Tooey' Spaatz.

In January 1944, the Eighth Air Force resumed the offensive with twice as many bombers as it had three months earlier. It launched a series of maximum-effort strikes culminating in the six-day Operation Argument, 'Big Week', in February. Maximum efforts by the Eighth and Fifteenth Air Forces against the German aircraft industry damaged

*Above; A mixed formation of the 355th Fighter Group Mustang escort fighters, 'bubble' hood P-51Ds and a 'razorback' P-51B in the background.*

*Right; 91st Bomb Group B-17Gs Fortresses, some in natural metal finish and others in the earlier olive drab and dark gray camouflage.*

previous summer. The first raids against the new priority target, the German synthetic fuel and petrochemical industries, were also launched, with good results. This industry had produced 175,000 tons of aviation fuel in April 1944. By September, this was down to 7,000 tons. However, directives from the Supreme Allied Command pulled an increasing percentage of the bombers' sorties into hitting transportation targets in France in preparation for D-Day. Bombing V-1 and V-2 missile sites also a priority.

On D-Day and throughout the fighting in Normandy, the Eighth Air Force was increasingly called on to hit targets near the front lines as well as German lines of communications and support installations. Then, the offensive against synthetic oil resumed in earnest. The targets around Leipzig were especially well defended. Other targets included transportation, aircraft industry, and administrative centers. While flak rather than fighters was now the main opponent, the Luftwaffe could still put in unexpected appearances, sometimes inflicting losses as painful as those of 1943.

# THE B-17G

**The ultimate development of the B-17, the B-17G retained the wings and the basic layout of the Boeing 299 of 1934. The rest was, largely, a different airplane. B-17Gs increasingly relied on radar bombing. They defended themselves against fighters with .50 caliber machine-guns in power-operated turrets. Electronic countermeasures (ECM) were employed against flak. None of these had been a feature of the original design.**

*Above; Two B-17Gs of the 533rd Bomb Squadron, 'Dream Baby' in the foreground with a Cheyenne 'stinger' tail turret, and 'Lucky Me' with a Boeing tail turret which was lost in September 1944.*

The B-17's basic design was excellent not because it represented state of the art technology, it was 10 years old in 1944, but because it was adaptable. It was designed when speed was seen as the bomber's sure defense in a pre-radar world. But even before the heavy losses of the few, turretless, early B-17C and B-17D models over Europe (flown by the RAF against the Luftwaffe) and the Philippines (flown by the USAAF against the Japanese), a major redesign created the B-17E. The first B-17 version to be a viable offensive weapon, the B-17E incorporated power-operated turrets and the Norden bombsight. These were soon followed by B-17Fs, with over 400 modifications, the most apparent being improved broad-blade propellers, a frameless Plexiglas nose and more forward firing guns to meet head-on attacks. The B-17G's most obvious external improvement was also to defend against head-on attacks: the chin turret.

Another obvious external change was the fact that, starting in January 1944, B-17Gs were delivered to the USAAF in natural metal. Camouflage paint added enough weight to the airplanes to reduce their performance: without it, B-17s achieved higher speeds and better fuel consumption. It also gave scope to colorful group markings on the fins and wings.

The B-17 proved a very robust airplane: the result of its early 1930s design which required more weight in the structure, hence its great strength, and less available for load carrying than later designs. The bridge-girder truss ribs inside the wing carried an internal corrugated aluminum skin, reinforcing the outer stressed aluminum skin's ability to withstand compression loads. Starting with the B-17E, the fuel tanks between the wing ribs were self-sealing, which reduced the risk of fire and explosion as well as 'hydraulic ram', the damage to an aircraft's structure caused by the fuel in a tank being displaced by the kinetic energy of a projectile. Ruggedness and ease of repair was key in the sustained high-intensity war of attrition that the USAAF carried out in the European Theater of Operations (ETO). Damage was so common that the B-17's ability to sustain it and be quickly and effectively repaired back at base was instrumental in maintaining the strategic air offensive.

Loaded B-17Gs cruise in formation at about 160-180 mph indicated at 25-28,000 feet (c. 8,000 m), higher than any other bomber in the ETO. The turbo-supercharger boosted engine performance, allowing higher manifold pressure for take-off and cruising at high altitude, yielding longer range and less vulnerability to flak.

In the words of one of its wartime pilots, Lieutenant James W. Johnson:

'The Fortress inspired a tremendous confidence. It was the only propeller driven aircraft I have flown that was completely viceless; there were no undesirable flight characteristics. The directional stability was excellent and, properly trimmed, the B-17 could be taken off, landed, and banked without change of trim'.

Even when losses were heavy, the B-17 retained the confidence of the men who had to fly it into combat. Wartime surveys showed that 92% of B-17 flyers thought they had the best airplane for the job, as compared to some 77% of those flying B-24s. While any wartime flying was dangerous, both in the US and in England, the B-17 had the lowest accident rate of any heavy bomber, a tribute to its flying characteristics.

# THE B-17G's WEAPONS

The B-17G's bombloads were normally less than those of its USAAF and RAF counterparts, reflecting its older design, the weight of its heavy defensive armament, gunners, and armor plate; and the size of its bomb bay. A 4-5,000 pound (c.2,000 kg) bombload was normally carried for deep targets such as Leipzig or Berlin, considerably less than RAF heavy bombers carried at night. For shorter range missions, heavier loads might be carried internally, and some B-17s could be fitted with external underwing bomb racks.

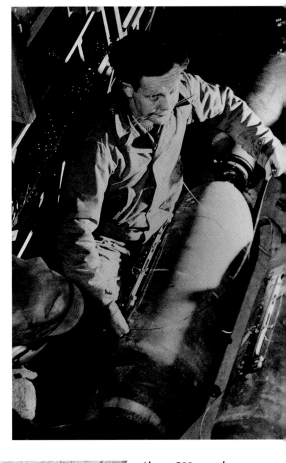

The main offensive weapon of the B-17 was the M64 500 and M65 1,000 pound (454 kg) high explosive bombs. Replacing pre-war 300 and 600-pound (136 and 272 kg) designs, they were serviceable, reliable weapons but lacked destructive power against industrial and infrastructure targets. A single direct hit by such bombs did not have much a chance of destroying factory machine tools or major structures. And it was difficult to obtain multiple direct hits to compensate for the lack of damage inflicted by individual bombs. The M34 2,000 pound (909 kg) bomb, which was unstable and hence less accurate, was normally reserved for fortified or otherwise 'hard' targets

The USAAF, with its emphasis on precision daylight destruction of enemy industry, had not emphasized incendiaries before the war.

*Below; Armorers prepare to load 500 and 1,000-pound bombs onto low trailers from the bomb dumps at a British B-17 base in the summer of 1944.*

*Above; 500-pound bombs being loaded from the trailers onto vertical racks in the B-17's bomb bay by group armorers.*

*Right: A ground crew armorer giving a final check and cleaning of the twin .50 caliber machine guns in the power-operated Bendix top turret.*

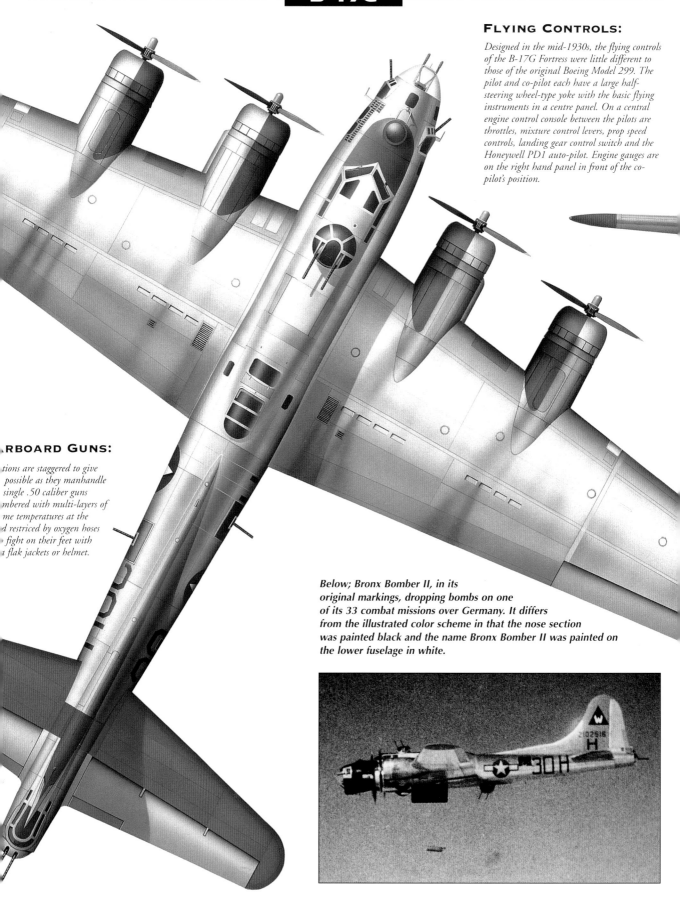

## FLYING CONTROLS:

Designed in the mid-1930s, the flying controls of the B-17G Fortress were little different to those of the original Boeing Model 299. The pilot and co-pilot each have a large half-steering wheel-type yoke with the basic flying instruments in a centre panel. On a central engine control console between the pilots are throttles, mixture control levers, prop speed controls, landing gear control switch and the Honeywell PD1 auto-pilot. Engine gauges are on the right hand panel in front of the co-pilot's position.

## ARBOARD GUNS:

tions are staggered to give
possible as they manhandle
single .50 caliber guns
mbered with multi-layers of
me temperatures at the
d restricted by oxygen hoses
fight on their feet with
flak jackets or helmet.

Below; Bronx Bomber II, in its original markings, dropping bombs on one of its 33 combat missions over Germany. It differs from the illustrated color scheme in that the nose section was painted black and the name Bronx Bomber II was painted on the lower fuselage in white.

# ALUMINUM OVERCAST

'Aluminum Overcast' was a Boeing-built B-17G-50, 42-102516, delivered to the USAAF at Cheyenne Air Depot on 10 March 1944. In April 1944, it became part of 'The Great Silver Fleet', 72 brand-new natural-metal B-17Gs of the 601st Bomb Squadron, 398th Bomb Group, which, under its charismatic commanding officer, Colonel Frank Hunter, made a mass flight to join the Eighth Air Force in the pre D-Day bomber offensive. The 398th was the last new B-17 group to arrive in England. From its base at Nuthampstead, it flew 33 missions in May through August 1944, mainly against lines of communications, V-weapon and tactical targets in France but also striking targets inside Germany such as Berlin, Leipzig-Merseburg, and Munich.

On its 34th mission, on 13 August 1944, with the 398th, led by Colonel Hunter, it attacked the railroad bridge at Le Manoir, France. This pin-point target required the 398th to do a 360 and circle round for a second bomb run. 'Aluminum Overcast' was hit by flak, and crashed near Bosville. The pilot, Lt. Weekley, and the rest of the nine-man crew all survived. Two were taken prisoner, the remainder returned to nearby Allied forces with the aid of the resistance.

Only seven of the 72 B-17Gs of the Great Silver Fleet survived the war. The rest were lost, as was Colonel Hunter: a stark example of how costly the bomber offensive was even in its final, most effective, year.

For this B-17G, however, there was a resurrection, of sorts, when its markings were selected for the restored B-17G owned by the Experimental Aircraft Association. Though now named 'The Aluminum Overcast' rather than 'The Bronx Bomber II' as in its original incarnation, this B-17G, though once shot down, may fly for years to come.

*Left; A Piper L-4 Grasshopper, used by the Eighth Air force for liaison and as an aircrew hack, parked under the formidable nose armament of a B-17G Fortress at a base in East Anglia.*

## PORT AND STA

*The two waist gunners' pos them as much movement a their heavy pintle-mounted through open hatches. Enc clothing to combat the extr B-17's cruising altitude, ar and radio leads, they had little protection other than*

## REAR GUNNER:

*Fitted in the Cheyenne tail gun position are twin .50 caliber Browning machine guns with a spade grip and a Sperry N-8 reflector gun sight. With an excellent field of fire, the sergeant tail gunner is protected by bullet proof glass and from 1944, an armor plated panel at the rear of his seat. Experienced group and wing pilots often fly in the tail turret of a lead ship to watch the status of the following formation.*

In its early missions, the Eighth Air Force often had to use British 250 pound (114 kg) oil-filled incendiaries. Later, the USAAF heavy bombers used clusters of incendiary bomblets, the M47, time-fused to detonate at 5,000 feet (1,524 m).

Pathfinder B-17s would drop British-developed sky and ground marker flares to indicate turn points and ground targets to the crews following them. A few B-17s served as 'bullshit bombers', dropping leaflets instead of ordnance.

The B-17G was well-armed for self defense with John Browning's great creation, 'Ma Deuce': the M2 .50 caliber (12.7 mm) air-cooled heavy machine-gun. A massed formation could put out effective firepower up to 1,000 yards range, though individual accuracy fell off rapidly over 300 yards, even with the reflector gunsights used by B-17G gunners. The B-17G carried thirteen .50 caliber machine-guns, with twin mounts in the chin, top (dorsal), ball (ventral) turrets and the tail gunner's position. Single guns were mounted on both sides of the nose and the waist, with another in the radio room, firing upwards.

The .50 caliber's design, dating back to the end of the First World War, was intended to be lethal against aircraft and light armor alike. But its ammunition, ball, armor-piercing, AP incendiary, and red tracer rounds that would show gunners the path of their fire (and help deter enemy fighters) lacked the punch of the explosive 20mm cannon shells used by the Luftwaffe. It was heavy: swinging its 64 pounds against the slipstream would exhaust gunners, and its

rate of fire (800 rounds per minute) was comparatively slow. Gunners could, with practice, squeeze off aimed single shots. Its greatest virtue was its reliability. The M2 as mounted on B-17s seldom suffered stoppages. When they did they could normally be reached and cleared, even by hands in thick gloves.

Eighth Air Force heavy bomber units fired a total of 76.6 million .50 caliber rounds in action; the Fifteenth Air Force, another 30 million. They used these to produce claims for 9,575 enemy fighters destroyed. However, on many missions, the actual total was probably less than ten percent of those claimed.

*Above; 500-pound bombs on their way to the hardstands from the bomb dumps after being finned and inscribed with suitable messages for their ultimate recipient.*

*Below; After the waist guns are mounted before a mission, the gunners will check them and give the barrels a final cleaning if required.*

## SELF-SEALING TANKS:

*The B-17G is fitted with bladder-type self-sealing fuel tanks carrying a total of 1,702 US gallons while some B-17Gs are fitted with additional 'Tokio' tanks in each outer wing which give an increase of 270 US gallons of fuel to each engine. At a continuous cruising speed of 263mph at 25,000ft, the B-17G consumes between 180-240 US gallons per hour which increases to 420 US gallons during climb out and full power maneuvering. Aircraft with 'Tokio' tanks have a maximum range of 1,850 miles.*

**Below: The regular crew of 'Bronx Bomber II', the original name for 'Aluminum Overcast', who were flying it when it went down in 1944. Remarkably they all survived and almost even more remarkable is the fact that as of 1999 the pilot Lt. Harold Weekley (the tall one at the back) was the only combat veteran B-17 pilot still flying a B-17.**

## TOP OBSERVATION WINDOW:

*The dorsal window is directly above the radio operators position which contains the aircraft's short and long -range VHF, and long-range HF radios along with the strike camera, electronic jammers and IFF transponder. Over enemy territory, the radio operator mans a single .50 caliber machine gun mounted fitted with a ring and bead sight fired through the open perspex panel. After D-Day, the gun was removed and the radio operator took over one of the waist-gunner's positions.*

W
2102516
H
30H

# THE B-17'S CREW

The crew, like the B-17G itself, was a mass-produced, quality product. The original small size and subsequent massive expansion of the USAAF's bomber force meant that there were few cadres to build around. But amateur airmen soon became deadly professionals. The skies over wartime Europe, especially in winter, are unforgiving. Those who made mistakes often ended up as operational accidents, frequently taking one or more bombers and their crews with them.

*Below; The starboard waist gunner take up his firing position in the close confines of the B-17's main cabin surrounded by amunition belts, radio lead and vital oxygen hose.*

B-17 combat operations required more than skill. They required courage. The first time the Eighth Air Force hit Berlin on 6 March 1944, it lost 69 bombers. The news was not kept from the crews: it was on the BBC, and the next mission they were sent back to Berlin. And they went, repeatedly, regardless of losses. They were not fearless men. In a wartime survey of aircrew 40 percent claimed to be afraid almost all the time, a

further 44 percent to be afraid much of the time. But in the end, only four percent of heavy bomber crews quit or were considered 'combat failures' including those who were, in the contemporary expression, 'flak happy', suffering from combat fatigue. What motivated them was, primarily, a sense of duty to America (cited by 59 percent) even more powerful than the desire not to let down their crew or unit (52 percent).

## Pilot and Co-pilot

The pilot was the commander of both the aircraft and its crew, which was usually known by his name. He was usually a first or second lieutenant, with captains leading flights and majors or lieutenant colonels commanding squadrons. He was, as pilot in command, responsible for everything that happened on a mission. Sitting in the left-hand seat of the flight deck, he would fly the B-17, together with the co-pilot.

As a fully qualified pilot, usually a second lieutenant, sometimes a flight officer, the co-pilot underwent the same training as the pilot. He could do anything the pilot could, and the division of responsibilities was usually worked out on a case-by-case basis. This could include helping coordinate fire control by the gunners in combat. Many co-pilots received their own crews part-way through their tour.

The pilot made it to the left hand seat by completing the most extensive air and ground training of any combatant aircrew. Five weeks of basic military training was followed by ten weeks of intense physical training coupled with classroom instruction. Next, in primary training, he would learn to fly, logging 70 flight hours in about 10 weeks on trainers such as the biplane Stearman PT-17. Another 70 hours at basic flight school introduced flight instruments and all metal airframes on aircraft such as the Vultee BT-13 Vibrator. 'Streamed' for multi-engine aircraft, advanced training was another 70 hour, 20-week course on twin-engine trainers such as the Cessna AT-9 'Bamboo Bomber'. At this point, the pilot was awarded his wings and commission as a second lieutenant, although some received warrants as flight officers.

He learned to fly B-17s, usually older models, at transition training, a 10-week 105-hour program. Prior to proceeding

overseas, he went through 12 weeks of flying at an operational training unit or replacement training unit, depending on whether he would be part of a new bomb group shipping out as a unit or going to be a replacement for an existing group. This stage was where the B-17's crews were formed up and wartime operations practiced, with an emphasis on formation flying. To cap it all, the pilot got to take his B-17 on the trans-Atlantic flight to Britain or Italy.

On arriving in-theater, a new crew might be sent into operations immediately, but usually there was further training for replacement crews at a Combat Crew Training Unit before going to a unit. The Eighth and Fifteenth Air Forces often found new crews' instrument flying and navigation skills inadequate and, when possible, imposed remedial training before permitting them on operations. Once a replacement crew arrived at a Bomb Group, it would often be sent on training missions to introduce the men to weather conditions which often proved lethal to fliers trained in the blue skies of the American Southwest.

It did not always work like this. In 1942 trainees had their advanced training truncated. Pilots with less than ten hours transition and no formation training found themselves in the left hand seat of B-17Es heading to England. But, by 1944, the pipeline was in full operation.

## Navigator and Bombardier

Normally lieutenants or flight officers (later in the war, sergeants as well), many of these were selected from applicants for pilot training who had been 'selected out' or 'washed out' at some point in the process. Sometimes, when shortages of these specialties loomed, whole classes from pilot training were turned out of the cockpit and given additional training. After the same basic and pre-flight training as pilots, both received a 20-week training course and six weeks of gunnery training. Then they received their wings and commissions and joined a crew at the operational or replacement training unit. On a mission, squadron, group, and wing each had a lead bombardier and navigator and their deputies. These were often captains and majors, able to lead formations. Lead ships equipped with H2X radars usually carried a radar navigator in place of the ball gunner and his turret as well as specialist navigators for pilotage and dead reckoning.

## Flight Engineer

Usually the senior sergeant on board, flight engineers were often selected from ground technicians, especially crew chiefs. He went through a 27-week training course plus a six-week gunnery course to qualify. He assisted the pilot and co-pilot with the engines, especially on take-off and landing. He was normally on the flight deck, inspecting engine systems at least once an hour. On combat missions he manned the top turret. He was responsible for ground servicing away from home base.

## Radio Operator

The B-17's radio operator was usually a sergeant, unless the squadron or group radio officer was flying. After basic training, a radio operator received a 20-week training course in operating and maintaining different types of radios and a six week gunnery course. He was responsible for the B-17's short range SCR-724N and long range SCR-533A VHF and long-range SCR-287A HF radios, strike camera, APQ-9 'Carpet' electronic countermeasures jammer, and identification friend or foe (IFF) transponder. When possible, he took bearings on radio beacons, at up to about 200 miles (320 km) range, and provided them to the navigator. Over enemy territory, he manned the single dorsal .50 caliber machine-gun. After D-Day, the radio operator's gun was often removed, so he would take the place of one of the waist gunners. On lead ships, the radio operator

*Top; A B-17's two waist gunners check and load their .50 caliber machine guns prior to take off for a daylight mission over Germany.*

*Above; The B-17F radio operator, with his equipment on the shelf behind him fires his Browning with a ring and bead sight through the open top hatch.*

## POWERPLANTS:

The B-17G is powered by four Wright Cyclone GR-1820-97 nine-cylinder air-cooled radial engines with General Electric B-22 exhaust-driven turbo-superchargers each developing 1,200hp on take-off and 1,380hp under war emergency conditions at 26,700ft. They drive three-blade Hamilton Hydromatic propellers. Engine management is assisted by the flight engineer, usually the senior sergeant on board, who assists the pilots on take-off and landing and keeps a watching brief on the engines throughout the mission.

## UNDERCARRIAGE:

The large retractable main-wheel landing gear and tail wheel of the B-17G are operated by three Eclipse of General Electric electric motors. The independent hydraulic wheel brakes are operated by tilting forward the rudder peddles. The landing gear can be raised at a minimum of 120mph after take-off. The mainwheels protrude from the wheel wells in the inboard engine nacelles during flight which assist in a wheels up landing. In the event of an electrical failure, each wheel can be lowered by hand.

## TOP TURRET:

An electrically-operated Bendix gun turret with twin-.50 caliber Browning machine guns is positioned immediately aft of the flight deck which gives it an excellent field of fire of almost 360 degress. Only the Fort's large tail fin restricts its arc of fire. Having reached cruise altitude, the B-17G's flight engineer mans the top turret and often acts as gunner controller during combat.

## CHIN & BELLY TURRETS:

The B-17G's electrically-powered Bendix chin turret fitted with twin .50 caliber Browning machine guns is operated by the bombardier using a remote control apparatus. The belly-mounted power-operated Sperry ball turret, again with twin .50 Brownings, is the most remote position on the B-17G. Ball-turret gunners have to be small as he has to sit hunched-up between the two guns for up to eight hours per mission. The ball turret can be jettisoned for a belly landing - if there is time. However, battle damage can trap the gunner in his turret with the danger of being crushed during belly landings.

*Right; The ball-turret gunner checks his weapons before mounting them and squeezing himself inside his restricted position.*

*Right; Looking down on the radio operator's firing position through the open top panel where he mans a single .50 caliber machine gun while the Fortress is over enemy territory.*

had to transmit coded position reports at intervals and maintain a constant listening watch for recall or divert signals, requiring a separate radio gunner to man the gun.

## Gunners

The tail gunner, ball gunner, and two waist gunners went through a six week air-to-air gunnery course after basic training, receiving their air gunner's wings and sergeant's stripes at its completion, and then joined the rest of the crew at the operational or replacement training unit. One gunner was supposed to have more extensive (20-week) armorer training. Time permitting, each gunner received on-the-job training to assist either the flight engineer, radio operator, or armorer gunner. Squadron or group gunnery officers would sometimes fly missions in the tail-end

ship of a formation to provide tactical warning to the command pilot. Lead ships often put an experienced pilot in the tail gunner's position to provide the command pilot with an eye on the status of the formation.

## Crew Chief

The senior member of the B-17's ground crew was a master or technical sergeant. Usually, he considered it his personal airplane, but had to let a crew use it for missions. They usually brought it back dirty and full of holes. He (and his assistant crew chief) and their crew of two to four mechanics had to clean it up and make it ready so that they could do it again. They could call on the support of specialists at squadron and group level to help with repairs.

*Above; The waist gunners have to contend with sub-zero temperatures, restricted operating space and virtually no protection as they fire their guns through open hatches*

# CREW EQUIPMENT

The B-17's crew's attire was the heaviest and most complex worn by any fighting men since the knights of Agincourt. In deference to the democratic sensibilities of the modern age, there were no squires to dress them, only a requirement (often evaded) that, underneath it all, the officers wear a necktie.

*Below; Inflatable Mae West life jackets and survival knives are the final items to be put on over a B-17 crew's multi-layered flying clothing.*

The crew would wear long woolen underwear under their normal uniform. On top of this came a electrically heated flying suit. Above that came an alpaca suit or fleece-lined leather jacket and trousers. A fleece-lined helmet (especially in winter) with earphones, fleece boots, capable of being plugged in and electrically heated; and leather electrically heated gloves over silk

liners (sometimes with a wool glove in between), completed the basic equipment. The waist gunners, especially on B-17s with open window mountings, were usually the only crew members to wear fully electrically heated flight suits. The thick gloves were often dispensed with by pilots and co-pilots to get a better feel for the airplane, particularly on take-off and landing. Especially in summer, the fleece-line helmet was often put aside for lighter weight helmets or service or overseas caps.

Over the flying clothes came the personal mission equipment. The oxygen mask, parachute harness and, if carried, seat-type parachute pack (many relied on clip-on chest parachutes in an emergency); and the Mae West inflatable life jacket. An escape kit with maps, compass, and gold coins was in a pocket. Body armor included steel helmets, flak vests, flak suits, and armored sporrans. Heavy, fatiguing and uncomfortable, they were normally donned only once heading for enemy territory. Many crews would not wear armor despite its effectiveness: two-thirds of the men hit by fragments while wearing armor escaped injury.

Left; Heavy and uncomfortable armored 'flak vests' and steel helmets are part of a B-17 flight crew's issue but are seldom used despite their proven effectiveness.

Right; The movements of this B-17 waist gunner in full battle dress including body armor and electrically heated flight suit, are further restricted by spent cartridge brass and belt links.

# THE B-17'S BASE

Each bomb group usually had its own base, or shared one of the larger bases with another group. The Eighth Air Force's bomber bases were built for them by the British government. Most were temporary installations reflecting a common pattern, although some were pre-war RAF bases. The cost, in money, over £600 million and resources (especially concrete, an average of 175,000 cubic yards per airfield) was commensurate with the tremendous size and power of the USAAF in the United Kingdom.

*Right; Three characteristic parts of the Eighth Air Force's presence in England, a formation of B-17s, the 'stars and stripes' and the omnipresent prefabricated Nissen hut.*

The B-17 had a tire pressure 50 percent greater than an Avro Lancaster. It could fly from grass fields but, fully loaded, required concrete runways to operate effectively. A bomber base included a main runway at least 6,000 feet (1,829 m) and one or two of over 4,200 feet (1,280 m). These were usually connected at their ends by an encircling 50-foot (15 m) wide perimeter taxiway. The perimeter track connected the handstands, open dispersal sites, often 50 or more, around the perimeter of the base. Where the taxiway and the runways intersected were wide concrete pans so that several aircraft could do their pre-take-off run-ups at the same time. Dispersed sites containing the repair and supply services, underground fuel storage, a firing butt for machine-guns and the bomb dump were located around the perimeter track.

B-17s were normally dispersed around the base perimeter on the individual hardstands. These could be revetted. The hardstands were ground crews' action station in all weathers. Ground crews often spent days at a time at them, and a mess truck would bring them food at meal times. B-17s normally only entered the hangars for major inspections or repairs.

*Below; B-17G 'Busy-Baby' belonging to the 379th Bomb Group seen on its hardstand at a typical Eighth Air Force airfield in East Anglia waiting for its next mission.*

The technical site usually included two or more hangars for the group. On most bases, these were temporary steel structures, 120 feet across and 240 feet deep (36.5 x 73 m), which could accommodate multiple B-17s for maintenance. This was the home of the sub-depot attached to the group, which handled heavier repairs than its organic resources were capable of providing. The next step up was the Advanced Air Depots at bomber bases, several for each air division. Aircraft requiring more extensive repairs than were possible on bomber bases were brought up to flyable condition (or, failing that, disassembled and put on trailers) and sent to service centers or to base air depots such as Burtonwood and Warton in Lancashire.

For take-offs and landings, the control tower was supplemented by flying control vehicles at the ends of each runway. Usually located near the control tower were the group headquarters, the operations and briefing buildings, a medical facility, and the support and maintenance facilities for technical equipment, including the radio shack, parachute loft, and armorer's shop. Elsewhere on the base were quartermaster supply

*Left; An engine change on the flight line. The 1,200hp Wright Cyclone R-1820 series radial engine powered all B-17s after the ill-fated Boeing 299.*

*Right; Eighth Air force personnel at an English airfield select toys for Christmas presents to be given to local children.*

*Above; English corn fields surround the hardstand of this weather-beaten 303rd Bomb Wing B-17G parked at an Eighth Air Force bomber base.*

*Right; Most Eighth Air Force bases were carved out of farmland in East Anglia, and in wartime Britain all arable land was used for agriculture.*

warehouses, and 'communal sites' with mess halls, bathhouses, often a theater, and separate clubs for the officers and enlisted men. On many Eighth Air Force bases, aircrew officers had their own club, where they could relax in flying clothing – away from non-flying 'paddlefoot' officers.

Multiple separate 'living sites' provided accommodation. These were normally in peat-heated Quonset huts or, on pre-war bases, proper barracks, to the envy of the Fifteenth Air Force, who mostly lived in tents. The bicycle was the normal method of on-base transportation, carrying personnel from living areas from barracks to mess halls to their jobs.

Most of the personnel on the typical Eighth Air Force bomber base were part of the bomb group, but there were also additional personnel, some 500 or so, to support them, under a detachment of service group headquarters and a base sub-depot which supplemented the group's own engineering sections. The group's ordnance and armament sections were supplemented by an ordnance and a chemical company, specialists in high explosive and incendiary bombs respectively. An MP company provided security. A station complement squadron, assisted by details from the group, kept the base operational. Other support units included quartermasters, medical, truck drivers, finance, weather, gas defense and other specialized services.

# THE B-17'S BOMB GROUP

Each B-17 was part of a bomb group, the smallest self-contained USAAF combat unit. At the height of the bomber offensive, there were 26 B-17-equipped groups in the Eighth and six in the Fifteen Air Force. The bombardment group (heavy) was the basic building block of US strategic airpower. Operationally, the Eighth Air Force planned its attacks and issued its orders in terms of bomb groups. Each has its own unit insignia and nickname: the 'triangle A' 91st Bomb Group were 'The Ragged Irregulars'; the 'square D' 100th the 'Bloody Hundredth'.

A group consisted of four (sometimes reduced to three) bombardment squadrons (heavy). Each squadron had from 12 (the original number) up to 18 or even 24 bombers. The group was commanded by a colonel, assisted, usually, by two executives, one for air (the deputy commanding officer) and the other for ground operations. The squadrons were commanded by majors, though wartime turbulence and losses meant that command slots were often held by men above or below grade.

There were about 500 flying and 2,300 ground personnel in the original, 48-aircraft bomb groups, increased in the late-war 72-aircraft groups: in December 1944 the 398th Bomb Group had increased to 1,000 flying but only 2,000 ground personnel . Each group (and, within it, each of the bomb squadrons) was divided into an air and ground echelon. When deploying to England, the air echelon of each bomb group flew, either over the northern (via Canada) or southern (via Brazil and Morocco) ferry routes while the ground echelon came over on ships.

The group with an on-paper full strength of 48 bombers would launch perhaps a third to

*Below; Seen at an Advanced Air Depot on a Third Air Division base. The B-17G 'The Gold Brick' of the 'Bloody Hundredth' in the foreground, looks in sad shape, but went on to complete 100 combat missions before returning to the US.*

two-thirds of them, depending on maintenance and damage repair requirements and the priority assigned to the mission. A 'maximum effort' meant a quick triage. Parts and ground crews would be stripped away from aircraft that could not possibly be made ready for the mission and concentrated on those that could fly.

If a group did not launch enough aircraft to fill its own combat box formation, usually 18-21 B-17s, aircraft from another group would fill in. Often, B-17s would fly in a composite box with the B-17s from other groups. In 1944-45, the bigger groups were divided into 'A' and 'B' elements, each responsible for putting up 21-bomber formations on alternate days. Two to six bomb groups made up a wing, which was a purely operational formation without administrative or logistic responsibilities. In 1944, in the Eighth Air Force, the wings were, in turn, organized into three air divisions: the First and Third with B-17s, the Second with B-24s, under command of the Headquarters, Eighth Air Force.

*Above; Replacement B-17Gs, recently ferried from the US await delivery at the Air Depot at Warton, Lancs, to operational Eighth Air Force Groups in 1944.*

# THE B-17'S MISSION
## PLANNING

**The planning for the B-17's mission starts far away, at 'Pinetree': the code name for Eighth Air Force headquarters at High Wycombe, Buckinghamshire, where Generals Eaker and Doolittle made their command decisions. Strategic direction, weather, the number of aircraft the Eighth was likely to put into the air, intelligence about the Germans and the targets, the situation on the ground; diplomatic factors –near misses against targets in occupied Europe mean dead friendly civilians – all went into the selection of the primary and the secondary targets to be hit the next day.**

The staff presents the options to the Eighth's Deputy Commander of Operations (Chief of Operations). The targets selected from this briefing would be presented to the commanding general. In the afternoon, with the latest weather information, the decision on the next day's target would be made by the commanding general or his designate. In reality, it is not the generals who had the final say, but the meteorologists. Twice a day, the Eighth's command meteorologists briefed the staff. The weather was the key factor in Eighth Air Force planning. Both the airfields and the targets have to be in the open. Some targets, such as those in urban centers, can be hit through cloud by radar bombing. Others, such as specific factories, cannot. If an unexpected front were to move in, the English

weather could destroy airplanes as well as the Luftwaffe and scatter the returning bombers throughout England.

The decision as to the next day's target(s) starts the whole of the machine that is the Eighth Air Force. It will certainly affect more than the Eighth. The warning orders start to flow, starting as soon as the decision to fly a mission was made, reaching the duty officers at air division, wing, and group level, each headquarters calling its subordinates.

At Pinetree and the air division headquarters, the planning staffs studied target maps, calculated routes and times. Bomb types and tonnage were decided after studying target photographs and identifying potential aim points. They co-ordinated the fighter escort, with join-up and turn-back times arranged so that the bombers were not left uncovered between relays of their escort. The RAF will be on call to supply escort fighters, air-sea rescue support, and to coordinate the flight of the bombers through Britain's air defenses.

The smaller wing staffs (the wing was almost exclusively an operational rather than an organizational formation) calculated the required take-off times for their aircraft into the plans coming down from higher headquarters, and how their subordinate groups would make up the wing formation.

At the B-17's base, the warning order came over a scrambled phone on a secure line to the group operations officer the afternoon of the day preceding the mission. It identified the target by a code number and specified requirements –how many aircraft would be dispatched and what they would be armed with. The group staff went into action based on information that was sent, as it was produced by the higher levels of command starting the parallel planning process, over the teletype to the bomb groups.

The initial fragmentary order ('frag') would out the fuel and bomb load for each B-17. This information was immediately passed to the group commander, his air executive officer, the group staff, lead flight crews,

and commanders of all the squadrons and detachments on the base. Each would have a part to play in preparing the mission. In the group operations building, the planning is a joint effort between the group staff and its senior aircrew. Some aircrew may fly the mission after spending all night preparing for it.

A large status board inside the building shows the state of readiness of each of the group's B-17s and crew. The first step is to make sure that the group will be able to put into the air the number of B-17s called for in the plan. The group staff matches individual aircraft against the requirements. The formation the group would fly, with aircraft

and crews, especially squadron and group leads, identified would be roughed out on a blackboard.

Based on the initial warning order, the group headquarters gives orders for how many B-17s would be prepared for the next day's mission and how much oxygen and fuel and what type of bombs they would be carrying. This starts actions all over the base, as all the different specialties that make up the bomb group swing into action. As soon as the name of the target has been decoded (it is passed in the form of a code number) the target folder containing reports and photographs of the specified target is removed from the safe of the group S-2 (intelligence)

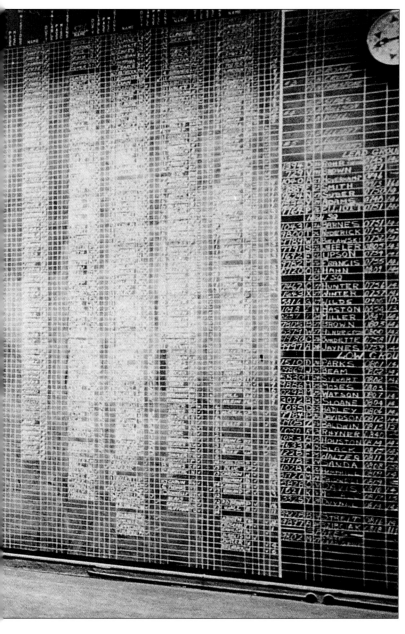

*Above; The big information board on the right gives the status of every B-17 in the group while the base plan on the left shows their location.*

radars and British 'Oboe' and 'Gee' navigation systems. The radars allow bombers to aim at the center of cities, but finding specific factories is not possible.

The group navigator officer could be called on to fly as the mission lead navigator, especially if the group was leading a large formation. In any case, he and his deputies check the latest weather data –teletyped to the group meterological officer–and spread maps and charts, preparing the group flight plan. Using their circular E6B mechanical navigation computers and B-17 flight reference manuals, they determine fuel consumption, times to take off, time to climb, and other requirements to make sure the group flight plan is consistent with those coming down from higher levels of command. They enter every change of course and the time each B-17 will spend on each leg (given the winds aloft predicted for the next day) into the flight plan. They also make sure of other details, also consistent with the orders, that they will later present at the navigator's briefing: call signs, recognition flare colors of the day, radio navigation beacon frequencies, check points, and other details. Copies, typed on onionskin carbon paper as 'mission flimsies' will be issued to each navigator at tomorrow's briefing.

The group radio officer is responsible for the radio equipment on all the bombers and it is his task to make sure that the pilots and radio operators are briefed with correct callsigns, communication frequencies, and code words for in-clear transmissions. The radio operators will be briefed with the correct codes to set in their IFF transponders. On those aircraft that are equipped with radar jammers and chaff, vital for survival by 1944, he is responsible for ensuring how they will be operated. This information all goes on other 'flimsies'.

Meanwhile, the staff take the never-ending series of clarifications, corrections and additions to the operations order from the teletype and, as required, update the plan and prepare the briefing.

The final field order from air division, which would often change planning made earlier, would be sent by teletype late in the evening. It would include the time for 'H-Hour', the time to start the mission that all the group's planning had been done around. The group plan is usually ready a few hours after midnight on the day of the mission. It is then briefed to the group commander, who may order changes, which must be made and approved in time for the mission briefing.

staff and duplicated for distribution to the lead bombardiers.

The intelligence officer and the group's bombardier and navigator officer will establish the mean point of impact (MPI) for the group and each squadron: the aim point for the lead ships. Other members of the staff identify landmarks, on maps and target photographs, which can be used to identify the group's particular target. This procedure is more difficult for radar or radar-assisted bombing. In many cases, if low clouds obscure the target, the group will have to divert to a secondary target or rely on the bombing of one of the group formation's two pathfinder B-17s equipped with H2X 'Mickey'

# FUELING AND BOMBING-UP THE B-17

At the hardstands and in the hangars, the ground crews work through the night to prepare the aircraft for an early morning launch. Fuel trucks, driving by blackout lights, come to each B-17's hardstand in turn. The B-17 is fueled through ten fuel caps, 2,700 US gallons (10,219 litres) in self-sealing tanks. Each engine's 38-gallon (143.8 litre) oil tank was also topped off. The oxygen truck checked and topped off each B-17's oxygen system. A truck carries K-21 strike cameras around the hardstand, with photo technicians to install them on those B-17s scheduled to carry them on the mission.

*Above; The bombardier arms 1,000 pound bombs shackled in the B-17's bomb bay by removing the safety wires.*

The bombs are loaded by the group's ordnance company at the bomb dump and carried on low trailers ('bomb trolleys' to the RAF) from the bomb dump to each B-17's hardstand. There, they are met by armorers from the bomb squadron who have already checked the B-17's bomb release mechanism. The trailers are positioned under the open bomb doors. Manual (later, electric) winches are fitted to the structure of the bomb bay. Shackles are attached to the lugs on the bomb. The bombs are winched into position, with the shackles attached to the bomb bay rack. 100-pound (45 kg) incendiaries are manually lifted into place. The two group lead ships are loaded with British-designed target indicator markers and air flares instead of bombs. Here and there, bombs are inscribed with appropriate greetings and heartfelt wishes. High explosive is definitely better to give than to receive.

Armorers arrived at the hardstand to deliver and, if time permitted, install the guns. Removed after missions for cleaning and to keep them from the English climate, each .50 caliber was carried onto the B-17. Ordnance men deliver machine-gun ammunition, belted into heavy 500-round wooden boxes, usually one per gun (less after D-Day), with extras in the radio room for long missions. The ammunition is hoisted into the bomber and transferred to the containers attached to the guns. Belts would have already been prepared in the specified ratio of tracer (often every fifth round) to ball, incendiary, and armor-piercing ammunition by the group's belt-filling machines. As they load the containers, the armorers run their hand over each round and each belt link, feeling for something out of alignment that may cause a jam in the air.

*Above; The ball turret gunner checks and mounts his twin .50 caliber Browning machine guns into position before take off.*

*Top; Ordnance men carrying a .50 caliber machine gun and 500 round ammunition belts to B-17s past a P-51 Mustang that will escort the bombers into Germany.*

*Above; A bomb trailer is positioned under the open bomb bay of a B-17G on the hardstand from which the bombs will be winched into position in the aircraft's belly.*

Above; Members of the flight crew assist the ground crew armorers to manhandle an appropriately marked 1,000 pound bomb under their waiting B-17G in December 1944.

Left: An ordnance man checks out the spent cartridge ejector chute under the twin .50 caliber machine guns fitted in the rear 'stinger' turret of a B-17G

Right; An armorer screws the nose fuses into 100 pound HE bombs shackled to the bomb bay racks. The safety wire will be removed by the bombardier after take-off.

Left&Below; Group armorers check and clean .50 caliber Browning machine guns, at least thirteen of which are carried by an Eighth Air Force B-17G, at the base armory during the night prior to a mission.

# THE MISSION BEGINS: THE BRIEFING

**The summons to battle once was the trumpet's martial blare. In1944, it was a soldier: the CQ (Charge of Quarters) with a clipboard in the darkness of 03.00 hours. The crews would have been alerted the day before that they were on the list to fly the mission that day. If the lead crews were not involved in the overnight planning they would already have been awakened, not long after the group commander was briefed on the plan, and given a through pre-briefing by the group staff and the bombardier, navigator, and bombardier officers if they themselves were not flying lead.**

*Below; The formation to be used and times for engine start, taxi, and take-off are all a vital part of any pre-mission briefing for the B-17 aircrews.*

The crews rose, washed –shaving was required to get a decent fit from the oxygen mask –and started the incremental process of dressing with underwear, uniform, jacket, and the fleece flying boots. The next stop is the mess hall for breakfast. Eighth Air Force bomber crews on mission days eat food the British have seen little of for years: real eggs, orange juice and bacon. For those without the

stomach for a big breakfast there may be doughnuts and coffee served by Red Cross girls at the briefing.

The briefing is held in the group operations briefing room, usually a large hut with auditorium-like seating large enough to accommodate all the crews on the mission and a stage. MPs at the entrance check the names of the crews against the roster. Crews mill around to check the plan of the base painted on a blackboard in the back of the briefing room. Each pilots' name is chalked against the hardstand or location where the B-17 he and his crew will fly is parked. Crews keep 'their' B-17 for missions when possible. A groan comes from one pilot, his usual B-17 in for maintenance, who has been assigned to fly one of the group's 'hangar queens', a mechanically unreliable airplane that spends more than its share of time in the hangars but has been cajoled to fly for this mission. He suspects it may malfunction on the way to altitude, depriving him and his crew of another mission needed to complete their tour of duty or, worse, something will fail over enemy territory.

Each pilot receives his flimsy, including the flight plan and a copy of the formation flight diagram, typed the night before by the group staff, showing how the group formation will be arranged, with the name of each pilot indicated. The crews take their seats, officers up front, enlisted men in the back. 'Atten-hut' brings the audience to their feet for the entry of the group and squadron commanders and the group staff officers. Those who will be flying in the mission are, like the audience, in their flying clothes.

Roll call: the pilots, in the front row, answer for their crews, craning their necks around to see that they are all present. The opening act at the briefing is often the security officer, with reminders about personal and operational security requirements.

The briefing room stage has, as a backdrop, a large map behind a curtain. At an appropriate moment, the briefer, usually the group commander or operations officer, will order the curtain drawn. The route the group would be flying that day would be shown in black ribbon stretched from pins representing checkpoints and changes of course. The route was not straight, and avoided known flak concentrations, marked in red on the map. Adding to the theatrical milieu, there would be an instantaneous audience reaction to the revealed map: groans for Berlin, Leipzig, or the Ruhr; cheers for less heavily defended targets in France.

The briefer identifies the target and explains why it is to be attacked today. The briefer then follows the black yarn along with a pointer, with more detail spent on the target. For this, a screen is lowered from the ceiling and the target photograph from the file is projected, as a slide, on it. The MPI, camouflage, aim points, landmarks for target identification, are all emphasized. The briefer's assistant unveils the formation chart, showing the group's formation that day and where it will be in relation to the other groups of its wing and the other wings of its air division,

Next up is the group intelligence officer. Usually a 'paddlefoot', he starts with the target detail, using the photograph, and works on to defenses expected at the target and en route. Some aircrew may have been fatalistic about the threat, but the next briefing officer, the group weather officer, has his listeners' undivided attention when he describes the conditions expected for takeoff (today: overcast), en route, over the target, and upon return.

*Above; All members of a B-17's aircrew pay attention to the briefing officers whose information and instructions may save their life.*

*Below; One of the most vital pieces of information for the pilot and his navigator is the weather forecast, especially that over the target area.*

*Above The group's B-17 navigators get a specialized brief from the group navigator officer who distributes maps and the day's radio beacon frequencies.*

The group navigator officer goes over the flight plan in more detail, including the fighter escort join-up positions and times. The group bombardier officer, gunnery officer, and radio officer provide specialist information: numbers of bombs and the delays to their fuses, ammunition to be carried, frequencies to be used. Callsigns and brevity codes for voice radio communication are reviewed. Crews are reminded of proper emergency procedures.

To conclude the general briefing, the group navigator officer synchronizes watches for the audience.

'Set you watches at oh-four-hundred oh four hours. Five-four-three-two-one-hack'.

The mission briefing now breaks up into specialized briefings for the different crew members: pilots, navigators, bombardiers, radiomen, gunners. The pilots go over the times on the flight plans they have been issued and the engine settings at each stage of the mission. At the navigation briefing, the group navigator officer distributes typed sheets of the day's radio beacon frequencies and their times of operation. He issues maps and typed flight plans, goes over the route again, with the time (after H-hour) of each change in course, the location of each turning point, and how much time and distance will be spent on each leg of the course.

*Right; The group navigator officer concludes the briefing with the synchronizing of all the aircrew's watches to the time that the mission will be run to.*

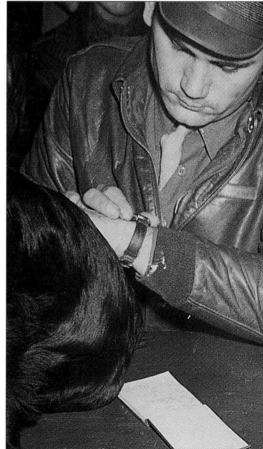

The bombardier's briefing goes over a photo of the target, with attention given to how the bombs are to be fused as well as likely aim points. The radiomen get their codes and frequencies for their radios and, for those B-17s carrying them, the instructions for the operation of their radar jammers. The gunners are briefed with the latest intelligence of expected fighter opposition. After the briefings, those who wished to could attend a prayer service with the chaplain.

After the briefing, the crew head for the flight equipment shop to draw their heavy flying clothes, body armor, Mae West, escape and evasion kits (which, containing gold coins, must be signed for) and parachutes. Each bombardier is given a bomb sight, to carry it to the B-17. Aircrew are ordered to fly combat missions without any personal effects or jewelry, an order often disregarded, but these can be checked with a property officer at the same time they draw their parachutes.

Sidearms, usually .45 caliber pistols are optional. By 1944, reports of the murder of shot-down bomber crews are widespread. Some aircrew pack an extra magazine for their automatic. Others instead carry a rolled-

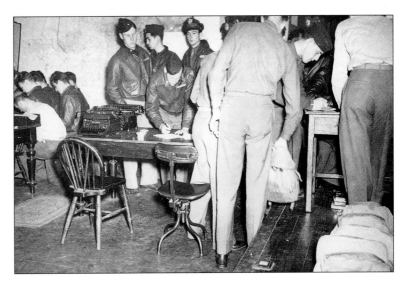

up London newspaper, not as a self-defense weapon but rather to prove to potential captors that they are not a spy. Some crew members bring G.I. shoes with them: their flying boots are no good for long walks if forced to bail out. Heavily laden, the crew boards trucks for the trip to their airplane's hardstand.

*Above; Following the mission briefing and specialized aircrew briefings, the aircrews sign for and draw their flying gear from the flight equipment shop.*

# B-17 PRE-FLIGHT

The ground crew worked in the open in blackout conditions through the night to make the B-17 mission-ready. They have tested the controls, made sure the oxygen cylinders were full, and run up the engines, disturbing others' pre-mission sleep. Now the B-17 waits for its flight crew, plugged into with a generator cart to provide external power.

*Above; Ground crewmen make last minute checks on a B-17G or amuse themselves while they wait for the aircrews to finish their briefings and collect their flight gear.*

The B-17's crew is dropped off a half hour to an hour before their scheduled engine start time. First, the crew checks their personal equipment. Often, pilots would inspect the personal equipment of each of the crew members, lining them up on the hardstand, and then have the co-pilot check their own. Before the remaining flying clothes are hauled on, the crew urinates in the grass around the hardstand.

The pilot consults with the crew chief and reviews the Form 1A, which sets out the maintenance status of the airplane and any work that has been carried out. The next step is the external walk-around inspection. Relying on his checklist, the pilot and co-pilot, accompanied by the crew chief, will make sure that the B-17 is ready to fly. He makes sure that any external gust locks on the rudder and other control surfaces have been removed: the original Boeing 299 was only the first of many that crashed from trying to take off with them in place. The Dzus fasteners on the cowling are also checked, to make sure they do not come loose on take-off. The four exposed turbo-supercharger wheels, in the surface of the underwing nacelles, are checked for freedom of movement, clearance and lack of apparent cracks or damage. Without the turbo-superchargers, the B-17 will not get off the ground with this load, let alone complete the mission. The top and ball turrets are rotated to the rear and locked in place. Everything that can be checked from the ground outside the airplane will be checked in the walk-around.

To enter the B-17, most of the crew use the main entry door by the right waist gun. A few exhibit their gymnastic prowess by pulling themselves up through the nose escape hatch, a stunt widely copied in post-war films. Inside, they are met by the unique smell of the B-17, a mixture of fuel and hydraulic fluid.

The pilot continues his walk-around inspection internally while the co-pilot uses the load sheet, including the details of the B-17's bomb, fuel and ammunition loads, and the slide-rule type computer that came with the airplane to compute the location of the center of gravity and fill in Form F, the weight and balance form, which shows how much the B-17 is carrying and where it is, to make sure it is neither too heavy nor out of balance. Completed, the pilot checks and signs the Form F. If all major problems have been resolved, unresolved minor problems are indicated by a red diagonal line, the pilot signs the Form 1A. Now it's his airplane, not the crew chief's.

The pilot and the co-pilot start the cockpit check. The first step is to remove the control restraint from the large half-circle control wheels with the Boeing trademark at the hub. They adjust seats and look around out the cockpit windows as they move the controls, checking that the control surfaces move freely. The three trim tab controls –for rudder, aileron and elevators –are all set at neutral. Out comes a checklist and, using the external power from the generator, the B-17's cockpit starts to come to life.

Each crew member has pre-flight inspection responsibilities. Turret motors and switches are checked. The flight engineer checks the engine gauges and the fuel and oil load. The bombardier will check the loading of the bombs and their racks, releases, and shackles through the open bomb bay doors. He mounts the Norden bomb sight, which he carried to the airplane. The navigator checks his equipment, including the radio automatic direction finding (ADF) set. The radio operator checks both his high frequency (HF), which normally uses a Morse key, and two very high frequency (VHF) sets–the short-ranged one can also be used by the pilot–and IFF transponder. If the armorers have not mounted the cleaned machine-guns, the gunners will do this themselves. They also check the navigator's and bombardier's guns while they are busy with their own preparations.

The bombardier climbs up from the nose, past the flight deck where the pilots and flight engineer are going through their checklists, and walks onto the narrow catwalk of the bomb bay, between the radio room and the flight deck. There, assisted by a ground crew armorer standing on the ground under the open bomb bay doors, he carefully inserts fuses, passed up to him from the ground, into the nose and tail housings of each bomb, gently tightening them with a wrench. With pliers the bombardier tightens and checks the safety wire on each fuse, which prevent the arming vane spinning and arming. Fusing bombs is a delicate business. Entire flights of B-17s have exploded in chain-reaction accidents. The bombardier also checks the fuse delay settings, which were decided as part of the planning. Instantaneous fuse settings provide fragmentation effect, while bombs to be aimed at factories receive a brief delay to ensure that they explode inside the roof beams rather than on top of them.

Outside, the ground crew pulls through the propellers by hand at least three times, clearing the lower cylinders of oil that had accumulated while at rest. The pilot and co-pilot, along with the flight engineer finish the pre-starting checklist. The rest of the crew, checks completed, strap themselves in. The gunners sit in the radio compartment. The bombardier and navigator sit in jump seats on the flight deck. This keeps their weight better located for center of gravity purposes and provides a greater degree of security if the aircraft crashes on take-off.

*Above; The flight crew check their parachute harnesses and equipment before boarding B-17F 'Jerry Jinx' of the 303rd Bomb Group before a mission.*

*Below; In the pre-dawn darkness a B-17G is ready to start number three engine with a fire guard posted and an external generator to provide power.*

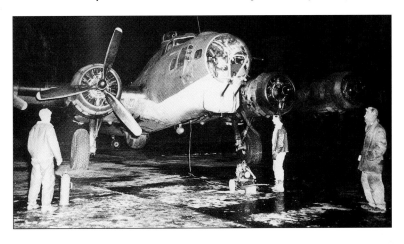

# ENGINE START

**Waiting to start engines, with the crew in their seats or sitting around the hardstand, is a common event in the Eighth Air Force, especially if either the field or the target is under bad weather. The carefully drafted schedules in the plans would all be slipped back as new H-Hours are set at 10-minute intervals until Pinetree gives the order to go or stand-down.**

Today, there is a solid low overcast over the base, but this is nothing to stop the start up, about half an hour before the planned take-off time. A bright two-star green flare is fired from flight control. The pilot, strapped into the left-hand seat, checks the flight plan on the clipboard he carries: time to start engines. The cowl flaps are opened and locked to cool the cylinder heads. He opens the sliding side cockpit window and checks to see that a ground crewman with a fire extinguisher is standing by, in case an engine catches fire on starting.

The pilot calls 'clear right' through the window and watches for the crew chief's signal that there is nothing in the path of the propeller for number one engine. The crew chief points at the number one engine with one hand while making a circling gesture with the other: the co-pilot primes the engine and then applies electrical power, provided by the battery cart. At once the first engine coughs, blows smoke and then bursts into life to 1,000 rpm, then is throttled back with its propeller ticking over. The nine-cylinder 1,200 hp Wright Cyclone is a particularly loud engine, especially when they are being warmed up. The rest of the engines follow in order: two, three, and four. The pilot and co-pilot uncover their inside ears from their earphones so they can yell over the noise to each other.

The crew on the flight deck check the instruments as the engines come to life. Another checklist: first: brakes. The co-pilot sets the parking brake and makes sure that there is hydraulic pressure for the toe brakes the B-17 relies on for steering. The build-up of hydraulic pressure has already announced itself by making loud bird-like noises in the cockpit. The engine instruments are all checked. The pilot calls in the intercom on all the crew to see that they and their equipment, especially the oxygen supply at each crew station, is ready to go.

Anticipation is as thick as exhaust smoke. Engines are turning all over the base. In a pre-planned order, the B-17s leave their

*Right; "Start Three". A ground crewman stands fire guard while a B-17G of the 91st Bomb Group at RAF Bassingbourn, uses the external power cart, seen forward of the main wheels, to start the engines.*

hardstands. The pilot watches the B-17s go past on the taxiway in front of the hardstand, waiting for the one that will proceed him in the formation.

When it appears, about ten minutes after

the engine start time, the pilot signals he is ready to taxi and, on a signal from the crew chief, the ground crew pull the wheel chocks. The pilot throttles the engines to 1200 rpm for 'breakaway' power to start the B-17 rolling, moving the throttle slowly to avoid a backfire. The crew chief signals, 'brakes off'. The pilot releases the parking brakes and the B-17 rolls forward out of the hardstand. The crew chief directs it onto the perimeter track taxiway.

# TAXI TO TAKE-OFF

Taxiing is difficult for a heavily laden B-17, ungainly on the ground and subject to weathervaning in crosswinds. The B-17 taxis straight ahead. The castoring tailwheel is locked into the straight-ahead position and must be unlocked for each turn. The B-17 steers mainly by differential application of the throttles to the two outboard engines while the tailwheel is unlocked. The tailwheel gives the B-17 a nose-high attitude on the ground and consequently poor forward visibility. The inboard engines are throttled back to idle. The outboard engines provide power to taxi at a fast walking pace. The co-pilot keeps an eye on the cylinder head temperature, oil inlet temperature, and oil pressure gauges to make sure that the engines do not overheat, especially if the B-17 is kept waiting for take-off.

The B-17 is designed for flight, not ground maneuverability. Planes are often blasted by the prop wash of those in front of them. In the crowded conditions, one bomber-length between planes taxiing to the end of the runway for take-off, the B-17 is frequently forced to using its hydraulic main brakes. If a B-17 should lose brake pressure, the tail of the airplane in front of it will surely stop it. The flight engineer or co-pilot checks the hydraulic brake pressure and keeps a hand on the manual hydraulic pump to ensure pressure is maintained.

The taxiway is filled with a slowly-moving traffic jam of B-17s, waiting for the first takeoff. Some are older, painted olive drab and gray, with many patches over past

*Below Left; Eighth Air Force B-17Gs of the 381st Bomb Group fill the taxiway at Ridgewell at the start of a daylight bombing mission over Germany in 1944.*

*Below; Every serviceable B-17G of the 91st Bomb Group is lined up on the taxiway at RAF Bassingbourn as they wait for take-off clearance from the tower.*

damage. The newer bombers are natural metal, with bright group markings. Most carry colorful personal names on their noses, with scoreboards of missions completed and fighters claimed recorded by stenciled victory markings under the cockpit.

The group lead bomber, an H2X radar-equipped pathfinder, heads the procession, followed by the deputy lead. They are the first to arrive at the last stop before the runway to do their pre-takeoff runup. That completed, the lead ship taxis onto the runway. There is a moment's wait and then another bright two-star green flare is fired from flight control. The lead B-17 starts to roll down the runway, picking up speed, as the crews in the taxiing bombers watch its

tailwheel lift and rise, followed by its main wheels. The B-17 climbs slowly away from the end of the runway until it is lost in the overcast.

The B-17s on the taxiway start to advance as more take-offs follow at one-minute intervals; any longer and the aircraft will be too spread out to join up into formation after they climb through the overcast. Several B-17s can run up at the same time. One B-17 does not take off but scuttles across the runway and heads back to the hardstand. Something is mechanically wrong and it will abort the mission on the ground. In 1942-43, often a quarter of the force would abort the mission in the air, even more on the ground.

# TAKE-OFF

The regulation one-minute spacing, half that in clear weather, for bomber take-offs is usually achieved. Slowly advancing up the taxiway with each take-off, the pilot is finally able to turn into the wind to carry out the runup, testing key systems to see if they will fail before full power is applied for take-off. Out comes another checklist. The engines are throttled back to idle, then, with brakes locked, run up at higher power. The generators are checked and the vital turbosuperchargers are cycled on-off-on. The propeller controls are moved between different settings, to make sure that the pitch can be changed in flight. At high manifold pressure, the two magnetos for each engine are checked, looking for an rpm drop as they are cut in and out. Then, each engine is run up with a short burst of maximum power. The propeller is set for high rpm for take-off.

*Above: A 91st Bomb Group B-17G warms up its engines at RAF Bassingbourn under the direction of its crew chief, M/Sgt Herbert Robertson.*

As soon as the runway is clear and the final checklist completed, about 15 minutes after it left its hardstand, the B-17 taxis the last few feet to the end of the runway, and, making one last, graceless turn, aligns itself with the centerline. The last few checklist items are quickly run through. The tailwheel is locked straight ahead. The gyro compass is set to the runway heading.

A green light flashes from the flight control trailer at the side of the runway. On the console between the pilot and co-pilot, throttles, supercharger controls, propeller rpm controls, and fuel mixture controls are all ergonomically integrated together where a single hand, palm down, could control them, helping make both highly loaded take-offs and holding high altitude formations possible. Grasping the throttle quadrant that controlled all four engines with the palm-up grasp recommended by the manual, the pilot smoothly 'walks' the throttles progressively forward to bring each to take-off power: 46 inches of manifold pressure and 2,500 rpm.

Rolling, the B-17 gathers speed quickly. The pilot and co-pilot keep it aligned with

*Left; 'Bacta-the-Sac', a 381st Bomb Group B-17G forms up above the cloud deck as the group heads for the enemy coast.*

the centerline using rudder, gently pushing on the upwind pedal. In a crosswind, the large fin and rudder cause the B-17 to weathervane into the wind as it rolls. If rudder action (it starts to have effect at about 50 mph) is not enough to keep it straight, the pilot will more quickly advance the throttle levers of the two upwind engines as well. The co-pilot watches the airspeed indicator start to wind up and announces the speeds to the pilot. The pilot has already computed his maximum refusal speed: the last speed at which he can abort the take-off and still brake to a stop on the runway–and minimum flying speeds. For a loaded B-17, it would take about 40 seconds and a take-off run of

over 3,000 feet (914 m) to reach the usual 110 mph speed for rotation. Until then, the pilot keeps the tailwheel back on the ground with stick pressure.

The pilot gently pulls the yoke back. The B-17 enters its element, all three wheels leaving the runway together. He immediately calls 'gear up'. The co-pilot taps the toe brakes to stop the wheels turning then flicks the electric switch to retract the landing gear. A moment later, when the indicator lights show the wheels in the well, the co-pilot announces 'gear up' and checks visually to see that the landing gear has in fact retracted. The radio operator checks the tailwheel visually and signals to the flight engineer as it comes up.

*Below; A three-ship element of 381st Bomb Group B-17G Fortressess on its way to Stuttgart on September 5, 1944.*

# THROUGH THE OVERCAST

As the B-17 reaches 150 mph (140 in clear skies) the pilot throttles back from maximum take off power to the climb setting with 35 inches of manifold pressure while the co-pilot reduces engine rpm to 2300, checks engine temperature, and monitors the instruments. The B-17 enters the opaque, gray-white overcast. The climb through the overcast requires every bit of attention of the flight deck. There are no rocks in these clouds, but there are B-17s that have strayed off course or lost an engine. The pilot's eyes quickly come inside the cockpit, scanning his artificial horizon, turn and bank indicator, rate of climb indicator, and airspeed. In the B-17 there is only one set of these instruments, awkwardly positioned in the center of the control panel above the throttle quadrant, so that it may serve both pilot and co-pilot.

The pilot flies straight ahead until he reaches 500 feet (152 m), then gently turns, using these instruments to guide him as he flies a pre-briefed course and heading. He feels the slipstreams and wake turbulence of the preceding bombers, encountered on his climb through the overcast (which is why the additional 10 mph climb speed above clear weather for additional stability). The intercoolers provide carburetor heat throughout the climb to prevent icing.

The B-17 now sets course for a 'splasher' radio beacon over which the formations will transform themselves from individual aircraft into a single fighting formation. The HF radio ADF (automatic direction finder) has been set for the frequency of the appropriate beacon. The pilot will rely on the ADF to point the way to the beacon. The white needle on the instrument panel pointing at its location. The pilot uses the ADF, to make sure he is on the right heading, checking it with the gyro compass. The navigator also cross-checks the B-17's position as they climb, using fixes on other radio beacons supplied by the radio operator.

Breaking out of the overcast is a spectacular sight: blue skies and bright sunlight streaming through high clouds. In single file ahead are the B-17s that had taken off earlier, still keeping their one-minute intervals. In the distance, other bombers climb from other bases, heading for the same or other beacons, gathering for battle.

*Above; 381st Bomb Group B-17Gs tuck in close to each other as they break through the overcast covering the North sea.*

*Right; Flying low above the scattered cloud deck, this lone 91st Bomb Group B-17G forms up into its position in a three-ship element.*

# FORMING UP

Some groups are led by brightly-painted 'forming up' bombers. These older war-weary aircraft are no longer flown operationally, but can still climb reliably through the overcast and make sure that the right aircraft join each formation. They are armed with a battery of strobe lights flashing the group's identifying letter in Morse.

The B-17 now starts circling the 'splasher' beacon, its location revealed by the swing of the ADF needle, in a gentle, standard-rate turn shown by the turn and bank indicator's little airplane wings being aligned with the first set of indicator lines at a pre-briefed altitude. Several groups orbit the same beacon, separated by altitude. The pilot looks at the tails of the B-17s already circling. He's flown to the right beacon: they are from his group. Each B-17's tail is marked with a group identification letter in a triangle for the 1st Air Division, a square for the 3rd, and a circle for the B-24s in the 2nd. Squadron lead ships fire pre-arranged flare signals to attract the airplanes that will be following them. If required, pilots use the VHF radio to direct following aircraft to follow them, but the whole operation can be carried out in radio silence.

*Above; A squadron of 91st Bomb Group's B-17Fs' forms up above the cloud deck over the designated beacon before heading for Germany.*

*Left; A formed group combat box formation cross over the North sea at 15,000 feet heading towards the enemy coast.*

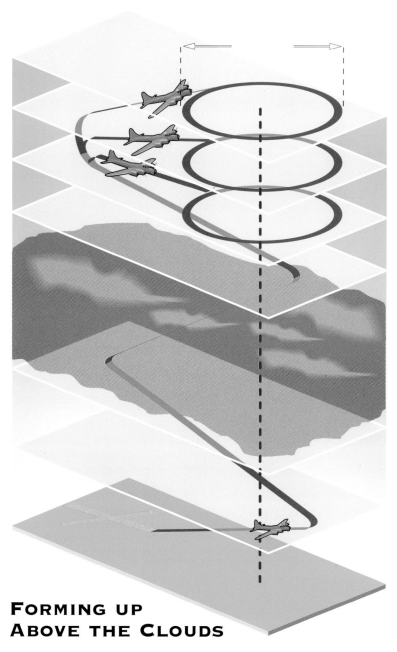

## FORMING UP ABOVE THE CLOUDS

**After taking off from its air base in Eastern England, the B-17 climbs through the cloud cover on a pre-assigned course, climb rate and speed to join its high, lead or low squadron which are circling at different pre-designated altitudes.**

The B-17 took off as an individual ship. It must now form up into its position in a three-ship element and into successively larger squadron (six-nine ship), group (18-21 ship) and wing (multiple groups) formations. The wing formations themselves would fit into the larger formation of one of the three air divisions, which, in turn, could be fitted together to make up the entire Eighth Air Force formation. An Eighth Air Force maximum effort, with over 1,000 bombers, could come over a target in an arrow over 100 miles (160 km) long and a mile wide or come home in a more compact mass, 30 miles long and 20 miles wide (48 x 32 km).

Forming such a massive force started with the smallest formation, the element, a three-ship 'vee'. Joining the circling around the beacon, the B-17's two wingmen appear, slightly below, and pull up into position on its wing. These two B-17s would have taken off immediately after it and, as they climbed above the overcast, would have kept it in sight. On forming up, the wingmen position themselves, as briefed, some 100-200 feet (30-60 m), judged as one or two B-17 wingspans, to the side and astern of the leader. This is close enough to provide the mutual support against fighter attack that was the reason for the formation, but not too close so that a single flak burst –or an exploding bomber –would destroy the whole formation. An important consideration was to make sure that the leader's slipstream, in a turn, would not hit the wingman on the inside of the turn and throw him out of formation. Fifty feet, or half a wingspan, was the tightest formation allowed, but this restricted evasive action and after D-Day flak was a bigger threat than German fighters, so there was less need for tight, defensive formations.

The squadron formation often did not correspond with a single bombardment squadron and might mix B-17s from two of these. It was created from the three-ship elements circling around the beacon. The squadron consists of two or three elements, with one in the lead and the others echeloned to left or right with 100-200 feet (30-60 m) vertical clearance. The element leads line themselves up so the straight line connecting the squadron lead with his wingman continues to reach them. A three-element squadron is a 'vee of vees' seen from below.

Eighth Air Force bomber groups normally flew in group combat box formation. Designed by Curtis Le May for his air division as an 18-ship formation in April 1943 to supplant looser and more vulnerable formations, it was modified as a 21-ship formation and, with variations, was used to the end of the war. The group combat box formation was constantly refined during the course of the bomber offensive and was changed according to tactical conditions, aircrew quality, and other factors. It consisted of three squadrons formations: lead, high, and low. The high and low squadrons would fly on opposite sides of the lead squadron, about 500 feet (152 m) above and below its altitude. As with the squadron formations, the formation did not always correspond with a single organizational group.

This was the most important formation and

maintaining the combat box was the standard by which bomber groups were judged. In combat, as bombers were lost or knocked out of formation, the formation would tighten up, following the lead ship and maintaining spacing between aircraft by moving into the places of those lost. These group combat box formations, usually 21 strong, operate for mutual support in a combat wing formation, usually with two or three groups: a lead group and a high (down-sun) or low group. It is a compact formation for defense against fighters. When bombing the groups will often shift into trail, the wing hitting the target one group at a time.

A wing may form around the same splasher, the low group climbing up to meet the high group as they finally move away from the beacon. The total time elapsed, from the first take-off to the forming of the wing formation at about 10,000 feet (3,048 m), was about one hour.

As the B-17 circles the beacon, the crew can see other formations forming up at different points around East Anglia, some ten miles (16 km) apart.

'Navigator to pilot, what outfit is that forming up to the north'?

'I don't know. From their formation they look like a bunch of Lancasters'.

'See any B-24s? I'd rather have the B-24s around than an escort'.

In B-17 groups, it was thought the Luftwaffe, if given a chance to attack B-24 groups which cruised at lower altitudes, would leave B-17s alone.

The B-17s of the combat wing formation

*Above; B-17s head across the North Sea for Germany. A maximum effort strike by the Eighth Air Force would involve over a thousand bombers in a formation over a hundred miles long.*

follows the wing lead B-17, flown by a veteran lead crew able of forming up 40-100 bombers. It leads them to their target as a single entity, away from the 'splasher' beacon, heading towards a 'buncher beacon' on the coast. The buncher beacons are lower powered, and are mainly used to guide individual groups home to their base. In this case, it is used for division assembly, where the combat wings, which have formed up in different locations throughout East Anglia, will join into their place in the larger formation. The combat wing does a large circle around the beacon. Other wings, joining the circle either ahead or behind as set out in the order. Then, this formation of formations too, stops circling and sets course across the North Sea.

*Left; The 452nd Bomb Group's B-17Gs show the stepped-up combat box formation which allows clear fields of fire for mutual support both horizontally and vertically.*

# CROSSING THE COAST

The crew assume their stations. The tail gunner climbs over the tail wheel coaming, reaching his bicycle-like seat and kneepads from which he fires his twin machine-guns. The ball turret had been empty and locked for takeoff. The gunner slides open the rear panel and curls himself inside the turret, his body between the breeches of the two guns, looking through the Sperry reflector gunsight. Their ammunition feeds down chutes from inside the fuselage.

*Below; Tell-tale contrails begin to form as this Eighth Air Force B-17F climbs to its cruising altitude of 25,000 feet approaching the enemy coast.*

In formation now, the B-17 climbs above 10,000 feet (3,048 m). The pilot orders the crew to go on oxygen. They slide on the clumsy A-14 oxygen masks, which they will wear for the remainder of the mission until they descend to return to base. Each crew member checks the oxygen flow gauge by his position and reports in, over the intercom, that it is working. This drill is repeated every 15 minutes throughout the flight.

'Pilot to navigator, what's the heading?'
'85 degrees for another six minutes, then come right to 110 degrees'.

The navigators that really matter are in the group combat box and larger formation lead ships and their deputies. The rest of the formation follows them. However, each B-17's navigator keeps up an independent track, so that they can take over a leader's slot if they go down or can find their way if forced out of the formation. The radio operator provides the navigator with position reports, obtained through bearings to radio beacons over England, as long as these are in range.

As the B-17 climbs, it gets colder. The temperature outside would be from minus 20 to minus 50 Fahrenheit (-28 C to -45 C) depending on the season and altitude. The cold is a permanent enemy. Bomber crews

suffered many frostbite casualties. One bombardier narrowly escaped death when a frozen sandwich, tossed in disgust from a bomber above him, smashed through the Plexiglas nose of his B-17.

Everything freezes unless heated. Fortunately, the waist gunners on many B-17Gs had their guns mounted in Plexiglas windows, not the open hatches of earlier versions, which insured that those in the rear of the B-17 were subject to a permanent arctic gale. Yet despite the cold, the passive solar heating can make the crew uncomfortable in their thick clothes. It is possible to freeze and sweat at the same time. Cruising altitude reached, the B-17 deliberately overclimbs its altitude by a few hundred feet, then precisely descends while reducing power from climb to cruise. The pilot and co-pilot move the controls in order: first, superchargers (to 28' boost), second, throttles, third propellers, fourth, mixture ('automatic lean' for cruise). Then the cowl flaps are closed and the engines take on monotonous but loud tone they will have in level flight.

The B-17G's electric turbo-supercharger controls were far more reliable and easier to maintain than the hydraulic controls on earlier B-17s. As with any piston aircraft with a turbosupercharger, the pilots think in terms of manifold pressure inches of mercury (measuring the air pressure in the intake manifold, which is 14.7 inches at sea level in any non-supercharged aircraft) to achieve the proper power settings. They also are used to the slight delay as the engines respond to changes in the throttle, due to the supercharger spool-up or spool-down. In formation flying at high altitude, the co-pilot's main duty is to make engine adjustments almost automatically, anticipating by a few seconds the need for power changes to compensate for the lag time.

As soon as the English coast is left behind, the crew tests their guns with a short burst. There is the loud, authoritative 'boom-boom-boom' of the .50 calibers, causing the airplane to shake and fill with the smell of the gunsmoke. In the waist, glittery cartridge cases and metallic metal belt links clatter out of the receiver and fall to roll around the floor of the fuselage. By the time the B-17 returns, it will be covered in them.

From the flight deck, the pilot can see another B-17 leave the formation, apparently with a mechanical problem or malfunctioning guns. A spare aircraft which has followed the formation to altitude adds power and takes its

slot, otherwise the formation will start out short-handed. Approaching the enemy coast, the spare bombers–about three to four percent of the total force–will either fill in or will return to base. After D-Day, improved reliability meant that the use of such spare aircraft could be discontinued.

The flight engineer checks the engine gauges, checking fuel consumption and comparing it with that in the flight plan. A B-17 burns 400 gallons (1,514 litres) an hour climbing, half that cruising, and the pilot needs to know if something is wrong and it is exceeding these figures. The bombardier arms the bombs in the bomb bay. Climbing aft from the nose to the flight deck, hooked to an olive-drab walk-around oxygen bottle, he sidles past the top turret, now manned by the flight engineer, and through the aft bulkhead onto the ten-inch (254 mm) metal catwalk that traverses the bomb bay. He holds onto the catwalk's supports with one gloved hand while with the other he reaches out to gently pull the safety wires, marked with red cardboard tags, that are attached to the nose and tail fuses of each olive-drab bomb. He saves them in a pocket in case any need to be re-safetyed.

As the formation approaches the enemy coast, those crewmen using body armor and helmets pull them on over their flight clothing, careful not to snag their parachute harness and Mae West or all that tethers them to the B-17: interphone cords, oxygen tubes, and electric heater cords. The radio operator turns off the IFF transponder as the B-17 leaves the range of friendly radar.

*Above; 91st Bomb Group B-17Fs seen in early 1943. 'The Bearded Beauty' in the foreground was lost on a raid to Schweinfurt on August 17, and 'Mizpah II' was lost over Stuttgart on September 6.*

# FORMATION FLYING

Once trimmed out, the B-17 is a stable aircraft. Its strong directional stability includes powerful aileron effect, especially in turns, and strong elevator control, especially during takeoff and landing. It does not need its controls manhandled. It does not have to be re-trimmed, even when going from climb to level flight or going around again in a missed landing approach. The B-17's stable slow flight characteristics are appreciated in the landing pattern and in keeping formation at altitude.

Because survival over Germany depended on the mutual support that was possible from the interlocking fields of fire of B-17s in a tight (but not too tight) formation, Eighth Air Force units prided themselves on their formation flying skills. While the B-17 is comparatively easy to keep in formation and did not exhaust the pilots, formation flying in the Eighth Air Force is never an easy process. The flying at this stage is the most difficult of the mission. The B-17s are heavy with bombs and fuel, yet have to keep formation as they climb from their forming up altitude at about 10,000 feet (3,048 m) to their operational altitude of about 25,000 feet (7,622 m). Precision in flying is key. A pilot needs to be able to hold altitude when turning or altering course, and not lose or gain a hundred feet while doing so. If the lead ship alters course or slows

*Below; A 'little friend' P-51 with 381st Bomb Group B-17Gs. By late 1944 there were enough P-51s available for some bomb groups to claim one or two to be used to lead them during forming up.*

## THE FOLLOWING BOX FORMATION

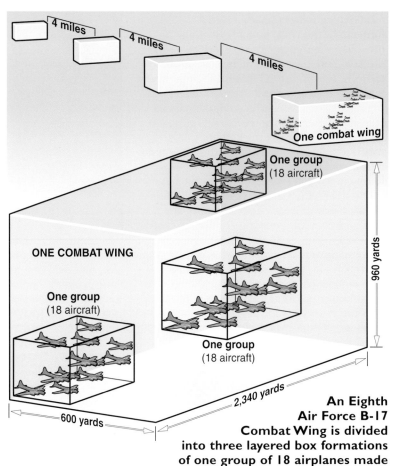

4 miles

4 miles

4 miles

One combat wing

One group
(18 aircraft)

ONE COMBAT WING

One group
(18 aircraft)

One group
(18 aircraft)

960 yards

2,340 yards

600 yards

**An Eighth Air Force B-17 Combat Wing is divided into three layered box formations of one group of 18 airplanes made up of six three-ship elements. Each Combat Wing formation is separated by at least four miles or twelve minutes flying time.**

down, it can send a chain reaction through the formation. This is felt most by 'tail end Charlie', the trail ship of the formation, which must constantly react to the changes of the B-17s ahead while contending with their slipstreams.

As the formation gets higher, the envelope between the 140-150 mph climb speed and the stall speed (about 120 mph with flaps up when fully loaded) declines. This becomes serious when a B-17 hits turbulence or the slipstream from a bomber in front of it. Recovering can bring the B-17 to the brink of a stall. This forces the bombers behind either to throttle back themselves or to turn out of the way. To avoid a stall, the pilot hitting turbulence may have to increase power, which, when it kicks in (the turbo-supercharger creates a lag in any acceleration) can send the airplane lunging ahead of the formation towards the tail of the B-17 in front of it.

With groups untrained in keeping tight formations–green units or veteran units like RAF Lancasters used to flying individually–these problems are potentially disruptive. For this reason, the B-17E-equipped groups in 1942 tended to fly in widely separated six-ship formations, a practice which came to a halt when the Luftwaffe started to concentrate on one such formation at a time. A disrupted formation means fuel and time lost to the need to reform. Over enemy territory, such loss of formation could be fatal.

Keeping formation takes all the pilot's attention, while the co-pilot scans instruments and also helps keep a look-out. They exchange roles at intervals. Except when on instruments, both pilots heads swivel around, looking at wingmen or for the enemy. If a pilot is distracted by anything –including friendly slipstreams and the enemy –letting the aircraft drift a hundred feet above its altitude or a few degrees from its assigned heading creates a real risk of collision or formation disruption. In the words of Colonel Budd Pleaslee, who commanded a wing of B-17s, 'When you look back from a lead bomber and see the formations real tight and in the groove, it's watching a tremendous feat being enacted'.

## DEFENSIVE FORMATION

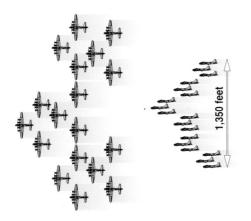

A defensive formation for six three-ship elements when flying over enemy territory layered within 1,350 feet for added mutual protection.

## 36 GROUP FORMATION 1

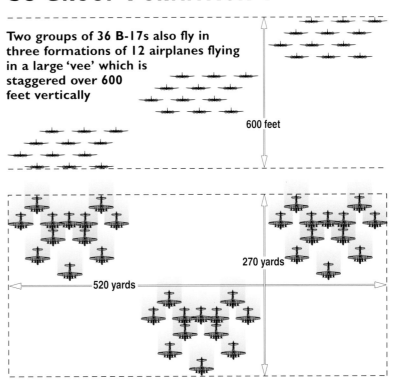

Two groups of 36 B-17s also fly in three formations of 12 airplanes flying in a large 'vee' which is staggered over 600 feet vertically

600 feet

270 yards

520 yards

## 36 GROUP FORMATION 2

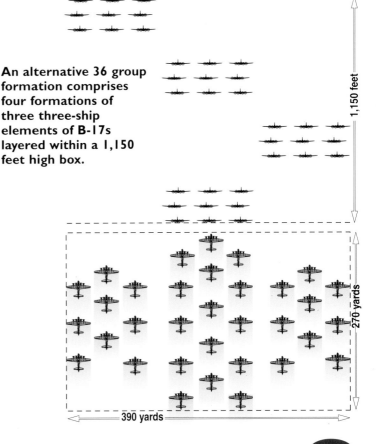

An alternative 36 group formation comprises four formations of three three-ship elements of B-17s layered within a 1,150 feet high box.

1,150 feet

270 yards

390 yards

# THE FIGHTER ESCORT JOINS UP

*Left; Masters of the skies over Germany in 1944/45 were the USAAF Mustangs which escorted Eighth Air Force bomber formations on most daylight missions.*

*Below; While from the 354th Fighter Group, a Ninth Air Force unit, these P-51Bs participated in many crucial air battles over Germany most notably those over Berlin in March 1944.*

**When formation flying is done right on this scale, it is a spectacular sight: hundreds of olive drab and silver bombers contrast against the central blue sky of 25,000 feet (7,622 m). Four pure white cloud-like contrails stream out behind each bomber, the spectacular but unwelcome product of freezing of water crystals in the engine exhaust. They serve as directional arrows, pointing to enemies for miles around the location and heading of the formation.**

'Fighters, eight o'clock high' comes over the intercom.

More contrails appear, moving fast. The USAAF uses a clock code for reporting the position, with the B-17's nose as 12 o'clock. The tail gunner has seen them overtaking the formation from astern and to starboard.

'They're Spitfires'.

The expected fighter escort overtakes the B-17s, flying in finger-four formations. Bomber crews' aircraft recognition skills were usually overcome by well-merited paranoia. The fighter escort knew the unwritten rule: point your nose at a bomber: get shot down. Only the fork-tailed P-38s were exempted from this harsh reductionism.

For the first B-17 missions in 1942, RAF Spitfires were the only escort fighters available. Their limited radius of action meant that they could not reach Germany. After the

*Above; 'Little friends' stream warning contrails high above a formation of 390th Bomb Group B-17F Forts on their way to a target in Germany*

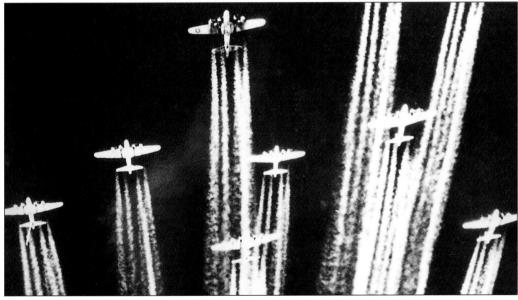

*Left; A frequent sight seen on clear days over occupied Europe in 1943-45, Eighth Air Force B-17s streaming contrails at high altitude.*

USAAF started providing its own fighter escort, Spitfires would escort bombers over the Channel and the North Sea. The Spitfires are relieved by USAAF P-47 Thunderbolts. The P-47s the B-17 pilot sees are those flying close escort. The P-47s throttle back, lean down the mixture, and stay with the bombers while being able to pick up speed quickly in a dive when a threat appears. P-51s, who will carry the burden of the long-range trip to the target and back, will use similar tactics. As the formation goes deeper into Germany, these will relieve the P-47s and, after the target is attacked, a second shift of P-51s will arrive to take the bombers home.

Because their economical cruising speeds are higher than that of a loaded B-17, any type of escort fighter had to zigzag to stay with them. Often they would have to turn for home after a short time covering the bomber formation. Even if large numbers of escort fighters were involved in a particular mission, they had to be divided up to provide cover to all of the formation as long as it was threatened by German fighters. It is often only one or two four-ship flights of 'little friends' that stand between the bombers and massive German fighter formations.

# USAAF ESCORT FIGHTERS

Loved by its pilots for its ruggedness and feared by the Luftwaffe for its battery of eight .50 calibers, the high-scoring 56th Fighter Group would keep its P-47s in the escort business until 1945. The P-47 was famously massive, with a deep fuselage and seven-ton empty weight to allow it to carry a large radial engine and turbo-supercharger. The P-47 was the primary escort fighter in Europe throughout 1943 and into 1944, when the increasing numbers of P-51s allowed them to be shifted to tactical missions prior to D-Day. In 1943 they carried only a single drop tank, and their radius of action did not extend far over the German border. In 1944, with two, larger drop tanks, they were able to range much further.

With its turbo-supercharger (the ducting for which was the reason for its large fuselage), the P-47 was always an excellent high-altitude performer. But in 1943 they were reluctant to follow German fighters 'down on the deck' and give up this advantage. By 1944, P-47s had been modified with a water injection system that provided additional horsepower, especially at lower altitudes. This and the ability to carry two drop tanks kept the P-47 viable in the escort role.

*Right; The reassuring sight for the B-17 aircrews, at least two squadrons of USAAF 'little friends' high above the Forts waiting to pounce on any Luftwaffe fighters that chance their luck.*

*Below; A USAAF P-47D with a crucial innovation - the drop tank. With a single drop-tank they could escort bombers to the German border in 1943 but much further when fitted with twin drop tanks in 1944.*

Lockheed P-38 Lightnings were never as successful over Germany as they were elsewhere, but were a critical part of the Eighth Air Force's escort force, especially in the decisive battles of early 1944. The P-38 was fast and maneuverable at medium and low altitude, but despite its turbo-superchargers, its performance suffered at high altitudes where most of the fighter escort battles over Germany took place.

The Eighth Air Force re-equipped its P-38 groups with P-51s after D-Day. (The P-38s had been needed to do close escort over the ships, because they were the one type of fighter the Navy could be trusted not to shoot down!) The Fifteenth Air Force kept them as fighter escorts until the end of the war, as well as using them as strategic fighter-bombers against the Ploesti oil refineries in 1944.

The bomber escort par excellence was the North American P-51 Mustang. The P-51 made the daylight bomber offensive possible after the tremendous losses of 1943, although it was not originally designed to escort bombers from England to Germany. Prior to 1942, the USAAF did not believe it would need escort fighters, as the bombers carried such heavy defensive armament. But when it became apparent that there was a need for such a fighter, the P-51 design was ideal. Originally designed for a British requirement for a low-altitude tactical aircraft, once it was powered by the US-built version of the British-designed Merlin in-line engine, its performance at high altitude was tremendous. Its high-lift laminar flow wing provided excellent maneuverability and fuel economy. The P-51's internal fuel tankage was large enough that it could get home from distant dogfights after jettisoning its drop tanks.

The problem of the need for continuous escort reducing the number of fighters that will be with the bombers at any one moment was to be in part resolved after D-Day as large numbers of P-51D Mustangs with drop tanks equipped the Eighth Air Force's fighter groups. With longer range, the same fighters could now provide continuous escort for much of the bomber formation's outward or returning trip

That there are P-51s available to relieve the P-47s providing close escort for this mission is a tribute to both the USAAF and the US industrial base. Though the long-range escort fighter was not the USAAF's original doctrinal solution, they embraced it when the need for it became apparent, rather than scorning it as 'not invented here'. The aircraft industry was able to deliver large numbers of P-51s after D-Day.

Formations of USAAF fighters, especially P-51s, were positioned between the bomber's flight path and major German airfields. Starting in 'Big Week' P-51s were able to seize the initiative and many times German fighters were attacked while climbing to altitude or forming up. Most of the work of the fighter escort is done out of sight of the bombers. Preventing formations of fighters from forming up into mass attacks is one of the most important missions of the escort. Many of the massed German fighter formations that were so effective in 1943 ended up fighting for their own lives against P-51s in 1944. The fact that the Germans must provide two lightly armed fighters to escort every one carrying rockets or heavy cannon into range of the bombers siphons away a large percentage of the force that, in 1943, had proven so effective against the unescorted B-17s.

## FIGHTER COVER

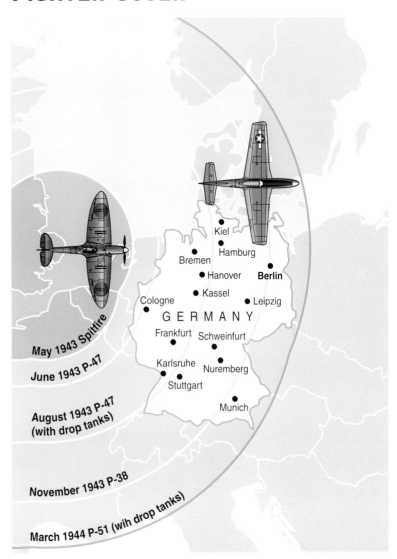

**The first Eighth Air Force B-17 daylight raids were carried out over occupied France in late1942 escorted by RAF Spitfire with a maximum range of 435 miles. In 1944, USAAF P-51D escort fighters could fly over 1,650 miles.**

The Luftwaffe fighter force never recovered from its losses, despite ever-increasing production totals. Jimmy Doolittle authorized returning escort fighters to go 'down on the deck' and strafe German airbases. Fighter losses were heavy to massive flak defenses, but it meant that there was no sanctuary for the Luftwaffe.

The B-17 pilot sees none of this, however. He prefers close escort, as he can see them at work. He also sees the damage done by German fighters that get through the escort. The appreciation for the 'little friends' is all the more sincere.

# ENEMY COAST AHEAD

As the coast of occupied Europe appears, so does the first sign of opposition: flak bursts from the coastal batteries. In the fields behind the guns, farm workers look upwards at the masses of contrails and know that, however bloody, much good will come of this day's events. At dispersal sites throughout Germany, fighter pilots sit by their alert shacks or already strapped in their cockpits. They listen to the *Reichsjagerwelle*: the broadcast radio commentary of the position of enemy aircraft and wait for the order. *Alarmstart*! the starter cartridges fire in puffs of smoke, and the FW-190s and Bf-109s taxi out for take-off.

The first German fighter the B-17's pilot sees is at a distance, a lone single-engine fighter. It paces the bomber formation for a while, weaving to watch his own tail against the escort fighters. The German makes no move against the bombers. His job is to report back the formation's position, course and altitude to ground controllers, who will direct the main striking force of the defending fighters towards them. In 1943, twin engine fighters would parallel the formation's course for hours,

*Right; A formation of Eighth Air Force Forts close up as they approach the enemy coast the gunners having test fired their guns over the North Sea.*

*Below; A Luftwaffe Fw 190A flashes past the wingtip of a 95th Bomb Group B-17F as it rolls off its head-on attack as the Fort approaches its target.*

sending reports. Some bomb groups, such as the 'Bloody Hundredth', were convinced they used high-powered binoculars to look for their identifying letters, marking them down for vendettas. Today, after a few seconds, the German must instead half-roll and dive away from the fighter escort.

His friends know where to go. Fighter controllers, watching the radar plots, are directing massing formations of fighters over the voice radio. Above their airfields, German fighter leaders, skilled, fatalistic men with high victory scores and low life expectancies, are forming their *gruppes* of Messerschmitts and Focke-Wulfs, many flown by green replacements into a *gefechtsverbande*, a massed formation for attacks on the bombers. It will be an uneven battle. By 1944 German fighter pilots joined their units with less than half the flight hours of their USAAF opponents: many were no match for them.

# THE GERMAN AIR DEFENSE SYSTEM

The Germans knew when most major Eighth Air Force raids were coming. Good weather over central Germany was almost certain to bring major attacks. Their radio listening service detected the radio checks at the bomber fields. Early warning radars along the coast of occupied Europe picked up the bombers as they were climbing to altitude and forming up.

*Below; Trailing contrails, these Eighth Air Force B-17Gs fly in a loose group formation over a target area obscured by German smoke screens.*

The word will be passed from radar center to command center to fighter fields, throughout an air defense system improvised with Prussian efficiency and honed in months of combat. The defenders were ready for most of the missions. Radar was the key to the defense. In the 1930s it was accepted wisdom that 'the bomber will always get through'. Without radar, it would largely have been accurate. Sir Robert Watson-Watt knew radar's importance when, on the night of the first successful test of his new invention, he had turned to his colleagues and said 'Britain is again an island'. This was proven in the Battle of Britain in the summer of 1940.

Though they did not know it at the time, the Luftwaffe found itself opposing a new kind of opponent, an integrated air defense system. Unable to defeat it, the Germans were able to apply many of its elements to their own integrated air defense system. However, they had to improvise their system quickly. Until the USAAF began to strike harder and deeper, in 1942 and throughout 1943, they did not allocate enough resources to the defense of the Reich.

Communications, both radio and commandeered civilian landlines, provided the central nervous system linking together the radars, the flak and fighters. Between the two was the 'brains' of the defenses. The 'battle management nodes' (in 1990s parlance) were in gigantic concrete bunkers. From there, the Luftwaffe directed the massive air battles of the bomber offensive, with fighter controllers directing formations over voice radio in response to a changing situation displayed on a lit situation map.

# THE LUFTWAFFE ATTACKS

**Through the cockpit windows, the pilot watches a staffel of Focke-Wulf FW-190s put on their own personal air display. Out of .50 caliber range, three finger-fours of the squat radial-engined fighters overtake the B-17's formation, passing them in a turning dive from above and to the side. Each flight is stacked up and staggered back to allow them to keep a better look-out and give maneuvering room if jumped by the fighter escort.**

*Above; Camera gun image of a Luftwaffe Messerschmitt Bf 109G carrying a 66 gallon drop tank, as it begins to break up under withering fire from a USAAF escort fighter's six .50 caliber machine guns.*

'Twelve '190s, two o' clock high. Watch them'.

Curving down in front of the B-17's box, the 190s change formation. All twelve fighters are in line abreast about two miles ahead as they complete their turn directly in front of the B-17's formation. This is what the Luftwaffe calls a '*kompanie front*' attack.

'190s at 12 o'clock high!'

Every gun on the B-17 that can be brought to bear opens fire. Everyone in the B-17 except the pilot and co-pilot mans one or two machine-guns. The bomber shakes with the recoil of the guns, filling with smoke and noise. Cartridge brass tumbles from the bolts of the machine-guns.

'Short bursts or you'll burn out the gun barrels!'.

One of the hardest tasks is keeping fire (and intercom) discipline. The intercom is full of position reports, curses, and shouts. The attack flashes by in a matter of seconds. A few seconds after they roll in to the B-17's twelve o'clock position, the line of FW 190s grows larger. Bright flashes under their wings, followed by more fireworks. These are 210mm (8.2 inch) rockets. The FW-190s now use their height advantage to roll into an

*Right; Many late model B-17G Forts used this modified Sperry A-1 type top gun turret with a reduced metal framework and improved visibility.*

attack with cannon on the B-17's formation. B-17s normally fly straight and level under attack, but have learned from experience that even limited evasive action can easily spoil the Germans' shooting.

'Evasive action, up and right'.

The co-pilot, seeing the flashes, already had his hand on the throttle yokes on the control console and now pushes it forward, pushing in more power so that the heavy loaded B-17 does not stall as it maneuvers. The pilot, with the co-pilot following him through, turns the control wheel to the right, keeping gentle back pressure on to bring the nose up. Coordinating the turn, both pilots step on the right rudder pedals. The left wing comes up in a bank –not much more than the thirty degree of a standard rate turn –and the B-17's nose swings to the right.

Heavily loaded with bombs and fuel, there is not too much the pilot can do to take evasive action. Nor does he want to upset the formation. There is just enough spacing between him and his wingmen that they can all change altitude and weave to throw off the enemy's deflection shooting. This has to be done with care: even a lumbering B-17 takes only one second to close the distance between a lead ship and its two wingmen.

The German *staffelkapitan* intended to force the B-17s to take evasive action from the rockets, disrupting their formation and distracting the crews while closing in to

attack with his fighters' cannons. At 800 meters, the fighters open fire, often while rolled inverted in the second before they flash by the B-17s.

One FW-190 pulls up and over the B-17, so close the flight engineer in his turret can see its underwing mud and gunsmoke stains. He rotates the turret by pressure on the left and right handles. Pulling on the trigger on the right handle operates the K-3 reflector gunsight, he frames the wingspan of the target in the illuminated aiming circle, but he has only a second to pull on the gun trigger on the left handle, firing the twin .50 calibers. He keeps his turret pulling lead on the fighter, calling on the intercom to alert the other gunners.

'190, now at nine o clock, pick him up.'

The radio operator sees the 190 flash past, and opens fire, pushing his single gun to the maximum limits of deflection. But it is a receding target and his field of fire is limited. One of the waist gunners picks him up too, but he has a difficult deflection shot as the 190 rolls down and dives away. Shooting through the formation, the FW-190s are difficult targets. In the words of flight engineer Technical Sergeant William Murphy 'the only

ones we ever got were those who made a bad pass and mushed off their speed as they tried to break away early or pull round on us. . .the experienced guys knew better and kept going through the formation'.

The pilot now must undo the evasive turn of a few seconds before he disrupts the formation. A quick glance at the altimeter confirms that the B-17 has gained altitude and is in danger of colliding with its wingmen. The controls wheels are centered and the rudder is released to bring the B-17 back to straight and level flight before turning back to the original altitude and heading.

None of the B-17s in the formation have gone down, but several are damaged. One is able to maintain formation on three engines. Another jettisons its bombs to keep up. Others straggle behind. These bombers may try and stay on course to bomb the target or jettison their bombs and head back for England, often descending to low altitude to try and evade fighters. Stragglers are at great risk. In 1943, half of the Eighth Air Force bombers shot down were lost after they had left the cover of the formation. In 1944, escort fighters would sweep behind the formation to prevent attacks on stragglers.

*Above; The view from the flight deck is spectacular. By firing 210 mm rockets, the fighters hope to break up the formation prior to attacking with cannon. The closing speed of the fighters and the B-17 formation's forward speed is over 600 mph. The attackers flash past in an instant, illuminated by the tracers from the bomber's own guns and those from the box ahead.*

# GERMAN FIGHTERS

**Defending the Reich were two major types of single-engine fighters: the Messerschmitt Bf-109 and the Focke Wulf FW-190, both in a broad range of versions. Twin-engine fighters included the Messerschmitt Bf-110 and Me-410 and the Junkers Ju-88.**

*Above; Trailing smoke, a crippled B-17 had been knocked out of formation and is on its own as an Fw 190 rolls in for the kill from 'six o'clock' high.*

The Messerschmitt Bf-109 had been the main front-line German single engine fighter since the late 1930s. Its design had evolved to near its limit by 1944. Faced with the heavy bomber threat, the Germans had up-gunned the Bf-109G-2, G-6 and later versions, but the drag and weight of the increased armament had reduced speed and maneuverability. In 1944, those used against bombers also carried underwing heavy machine-guns or 20 mm cannon in external mountings.

The Focke Wulf FW-190A was introduced in 1941 and outclassed the Spitfires and Hurricanes then in service with the RAF. But by 1944 it had failed to keep up with the performance advances in Allied fighters. Its performance dropped off at high altitude, putting it at a disadvantage when having to engage fighter escorts. More robust than the Bf-109, it carried the brunt of German single-engine fighter attacks on bombers. Versions such as the FW-190A-8 carried additional armor plate and sometimes as many as four extra 20 mm cannon under the wings, but this reduced their speed and maneuverability to such an extent that they were highly vulnerable to USAAF fighters and had to be escorted themselves.

German twin-engine fighters carried enough firepower to have a good chance of destroying a B-17. The Messerschmitt Bf-110 was designed, pre-war, as a long-range offensive fighter, intended to escort German bombers. Although defeated in the Battle of Britain, it proved adaptable to defensive tasks, most notably as a night fighter. Bf-110s also served as day fighters. The heavy firepower of the Bf-110G versions with two 30 mm cannon accounted for many bombers in 1943. By 1944, however, it was itself highly vulnerable to long-range escort fighters.

The Junkers Ju-88C was the day fighter version of the Luftwaffe's versatile twin-engine bomber. Ju-88s were effective against unescorted bombers in 1943, but after D-Day, they rarely operated in daylight, even with their own escorts, and the remaining units converted to single-seat fighters. But even if they are more vulnerable, the twin-engine fighters in 1944 are better armed than they had been the year before and can still inflict painful losses: in July 1944, a staffel of Me-410s decimated a B-24 group without loss over Budapest.

The fighter that was most lethal to B-17s –the jet-propelled Messerschmitt Me-262 –did not appear in action until the autumn of 1944, and then only in small numbers. After that, especially in March-April 1945, three-ship flights of Me-262s used their high speed and concentrated armament of four nose-mounted 30 mm cannon to carry out 'roller

## B-17 v FW 190

**Special 'Storm' units were equipped with Focke-Wulf Fw 190A-5 fighters fitted with two 20mm and two 30mm wing cannon and additional armour to engage the swarming USAAF day bomber formations in 1943/4.**

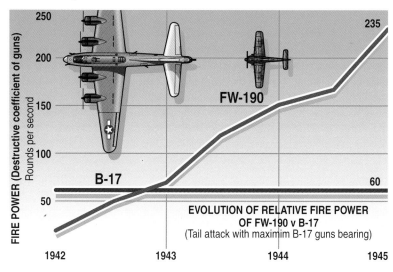

EVOLUTION OF RELATIVE FIRE POWER OF FW-190 v B-17
(Tail attack with maximim B-17 guns bearing)

coaster' attacks against bomber formations. Even more fortunately, they did not start to receive their planned armament of twenty-four R4M 55 mm (2.1 inch) unguided rockets until the last days of the war. These had the potential to be highly lethal against bombers in formations, and would have revived the head-on attack as the anti-bomber tactic of choice.

By 1944, Luftwaffe tactics emphasized tail attacks on bomber formations rather than the head-on attacks that had proven successful in 1943. The Luftwaffe reckoned that their chances of hitting a vital spot were much greater from head-on, aiming at the cockpit, inner engines, and wing fuel tanks. Only one of the B-17's 27 pieces of armor plate and numerous flak curtains is positioned to protect the flight deck from a head-on attack. The bulkhead between the nose compartment and the flight deck is armored, but this had little benefit on most attacks. Despite using self-sealing fuel tanks, the B-17 never lost its tendency to catch fire if hit, despite the improved engine fire extinguisher system introduced with the B-17G series.

## GUN EFFECTS

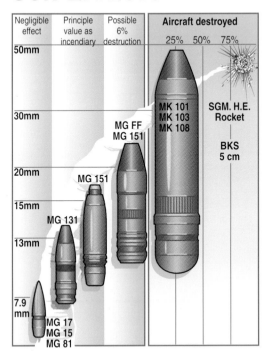

**The effectiveness of B-17 kills by German fighters depended largely on their armamant, ranging from the Bf 109's MG 17 7.9mm machine gun to the jet-powered Me 262's MK 108 30mm cannon.**

The Germans estimated that, even when carefully aimed, their fighters' cannon armament scored about two percent hits. In the one-second or half-second burst delivered in a head-on attack, a German fighter did not have a high probability of scoring enough hits to be lethal. They were hoping for a lucky hit to knock the bomber out of formation. The Germans claimed that only four or five 20 mm hits or a single 30 mm hit were sufficient to bring down a B-17 in a head-on attack, compared to twenty 20 mm or three 30 mm hits from the rear. Because a head-on attack limited them to a one-second or half-second bursts, even an up-gunned single engine fighter was unable to land a lethal punch. They just did not have time to adjust their aim and hit the target before flashing past. If a fighter did not break off a head-on attack by 100 meters range, a collision with its target was likely, with one or more often occurring on hard-fought missions Even in their 1943 victories, it still took an average of ten German single engine fighter sorties to kill a USAAF heavy bomber.

*Above; Caught in the gun sights of the fighter escort, a two-seat Luftwaffe Me 410 is seen in its death throes. The crew has already jettisoned the canopy prior to bail-out.*

*Below; A similar fate awaits this German Ju 88 fighter as hits from a P-51 escort register on the engine and flames engulf the wing tanks.*

# THE IP AND THE BOMB RUN

The initial point (IP) is where the bomber formation turns to make its bomb run to the target. It is usually a geographical feature that can be easily identified, ideally both visually and on radar. Often, it will by marked by red flares dropped by the pathfinder bombers. Intended to be about four minutes' run from the target, this means the IP is about 20 miles (32 km) distant for a downwind bomb run and some 12-15 miles (c.20 km) for an upwind bomb run. It is usually a hard, racking turn, intended to keep the enemy guessing about the formation's ultimate destination until the last possible minute. If there are multiple aim points or bombing altitudes, the IP may have to be further offset to allow the formation more time to divide and maneuver.

*Below; Two B-17G Pathfinders of the 96th Bomb Group begin their bomb run in close formation for mutual protection with bomb bay doors open.*

The weather over the target is good. The bombing can go ahead, as briefed, visually. Had the formation been forced by weather to divert to the secondary target –after D-Day, a Weather Scouting Force flight of P-51s would have preceded them to check conditions –the decision would have been made by the

command pilot and a coded radio message would have been passed from the radio operator on the lead ship and relayed throughout the formations, along with the firing of color-coded flares. Today, the lead ships have turned on their pre-briefed course to the target.

The navigator provides the pilot with position reports every 15 minutes. He will also tell him to make required course changes, giving him two minutes advance warning so that he can 'lead' the turn.

'Navigator to pilot, turn left to course zero-one-five in two minutes'.

'Zero-one-five, roger'.

The navigator has used a combination of pilotage and dead reckoning to get the B-17 to the point where it will turn to follow the preceding groups to the target, using estimated winds aloft and the E6B computer to come up with new headings. Pure dead

reckoning was highly inaccurate under wartime conditions due to the uncertainty of knowing winds aloft over Germany and the variations in speed and doglegs often required by formation flying. It has to be checked with observation of features on the ground or, above the overcast, by following the pathfinder B-17s with their H2X radar and British-designed Oboe and Gee radio navigation systems. The navigator uses a Weems plotter and the mechanical computer to compute ground speeds and winds and continually update and revise his flight plan from that originally given at the navigation briefing, using his collection of maps and charts and the gyro and magnetic compass indicators mounted on the nose bulkhead.

The bomber force may have to carry out a formation change even while under attack. If the tactical situation permits, groups coming over the target tighten formation to reduce the dispersion of the bombs, the trailing squadron leads throttling up to close the distance with the lead squadron. Bomber formations could

also be briefed to change altitude for bombing, often climbing to protect themselves against flak. It was reckoned that every 5,000 feet (1,524 m) of altitude above 10,000 feet (3,048 m) halved flak effectiveness. But it also reduced bombing accuracy. All else being equal, B-17s bombing from 27,000 feet (8,231 m) would have a quarter the number of bombs within 1,000 feet (304 m) of the target as those bombing from 18,000 feet (5,487 m).

The high and low group formations of each combat wing shook out into single file. Sometimes, the different wing formations would fly parallel courses converging at the target, or, (especially after D-Day), the entire bomber force would go into a single file of groups as it passed the IP. Originally, the idea was that each group will be over the target for less than two minutes, but combat experience showed that longer time over the target could yield more accurate bombing.

Target identification after the IP matched landmarks pointed out at the briefing with those identified by the B-17's crew. Visual bombing could strike specific factories, while radar bombing was only effective against large built-up areas. Visual target identification was necessarily key to daylight, precision bombing, but on many occasions, visual bombing was made impossible by the unexpected appearance of cloud cover or a smokescreen. This would, in many cases, require the entire raid to divert to an alternate target or hit the primary through the less-accurate radar bombing. But even if there was perfect visibility, the first groups over the target would soon cover it in smoke and dust from the bomb detonations and resulting fires. The lead ships would drop British-developed ground marker flares as aim points to counter this.

*Above; Smoke markers are dropped over Berlin from a group lead B-17 to indicate an aim point for the following formation.*

# FLAK

Coming off the IP, the pilot sees thick roiling puffs of black smoke appear in front of the lead group as it approaches the target. These are the explosions of time-fused shells fired from the flak: the German anti-aircraft guns. At its worse, over Berlin, Leipzig, or Merseburg, there are so many shells constantly bursting that it appears to be what the bombers crews call 'flak you can walk on'.

*Above; It was important for the B-17 group to maintain an accurate combat box formation as it flies its bomb run dropping 'window' and 'carpet' to jam the flak gunner's fire control radars.*

One of the waist gunners, responding to an intercom call by the navigator, leaves his gun. Kneeling by a chute installed near the rear exit door, he checks his watch and, at a pre-briefed interval, reaches into a storage box next to the chute, picks up a cardboard-

wrapped bundle of pre-cut aluminum strips and pushes it through the chute and out into the slipstream, a process he repeats several times as the B-17G flies its bomb run. Smaller drops of 'window' (chaff), such as this on the bomb run, could create false 'targets' which would be used by the fire control computers to set the solution rather than the real target aircraft.

The radio operator turns on the 'Carpet' radar jammer, having already set it to a pre-briefed frequency. Large numbers of bombers are fitted with 'Carpet' barrage radar jammers, intended to jam flak fire control radars and force them to rely on less accurate optical systems. Together, 'window' and jammers reduced losses to flak by up to two-thirds.

The B-17 will not fly straight and level for more seconds than its altitude in thousands of feet before turning. The pilot and co-pilot together are constantly turning at least six degrees, sometimes as many as fifteen, first one way, then the other.

The flak bursts are silent to the crew on board the B-17: 'if you hear it, it's got you'. But bursts are getting close, and the B-17 rolls from the concussion. A flak burst within 50 feet (15 m) will spray the B-17 with steel balls and shell fragments. The 'ping' of shrapnel will get the crew's full attention even over the roar of the engines, sounding to the crew like rocks thrown on a tin roof. As the formation comes over the target, the pilot sees, in the preceding formation, a bright flash, first yellow then red, then black smoke. A B-17 has taken a direct flak hit in the bomb bay, setting off a secondary explosion. All that is left is aluminum rain and one large piece of airplane.

*Right; The 379th Bomb Group would form up on an old disarmed B-17E, 'The Birmingham Blitzkrieg' used on the first 1942 Rouen mission, and also used for target towing and transport duties.*

# THE FLAK DEFENSES

After the defeat of the German fighter force in the opening months of 1944, the main opposition of the USAAF –bombers, fighters, and transports alike– was German flak. By 1944, as the German fighter force has proven less able to defend the Reich, the flak defenses were increased to compensate. For a flak shell to reach 25,000 feet (7,621 m) at its maximum slant range of over five miles (8 km) took 25 seconds, in which time the B-17 will have traveled a mile and a half. The Germans have to either predict where the B-17 will be in 25 seconds or, as they did at Leipzig, simply give up on individual aimed fire and just try to surround the target with a constant wall of metal.

The wall is very real. By 1944, flak damage was widespread in the Eighth Air Force. On Mission 250, the first strike on Berlin on 6 March, almost half the returning bombers had flak damage. After D-Day, especially during the raids on the petrochemical targets, often even higher percentages are damaged.

*Right; A few thousand feet can be a life saver as shown by this B-17G of the Fifteenth Air Force's 301st Bomb Group with flak bursting well below it.*

The main heavy anti-aircraft artillery piece was the legendary '88', the 88 mm Flak 36. The 88 mm (3.46 in) had an effective slant range of about 9,000 yards (8,226 m) and an effective ceiling of about 20,000 feet (6,097 m). The shells are detonated by an automatically set clockwork time fuse, lethal within 30 yards and 88 shell can inflict damage out to 200 yards. Each battery was intended to be remotely aimed and fired by an optical director such as the Kommandogerat 36 which used an optical rangefinder linked to a mechanical computer

*Below; A flak shell explodes perilously close to these B-17s. The explosion would not be heard inside the aircraft unless it scored a direct hit. However, the rattle of shrapnel hitting the airframe was clearly audible.*

to determine the range to the airplane, where it will be when the battery's shells arrive (if its flies straight and level), how long the shells will take to arrive (so that the fuses can be set), and the elevation and azimuth each gun of the battery needed to be set at to do this. The whole procedure to engage a target, until the firing circuits were closed, took some 20-30 seconds, about the same as the shells' flight time to detonation. If done properly, a salvo of shells will create a lethal envelope 60 yards in diameter around the predicted point of impact. Starting in 1941, the Germans also used a Wurzburg fire control radar to provide the inputs into the computer. This allowed accurate fire at night or through clouds. However, the effects of widespread use of Window and Carpet to jam radars and the German shortage of optics and fire control equipment served to reduce the individual effectiveness of German flak. There was also a chronic shortage of trained personnel: by 1944 flak batteries made much use of local teenagers and impressed Russian prisoners-of-war. The Germans compensated for this by massing flak around key objectives.

Supplementing the '88's were a smaller number of longer-ranged 105 mm (4.1 inch) flak guns. Defending Berlin and Leipzig were a limited number of an even larger 128 mm (5 inch) guns. Even Eighth Air Force bomber formations could not fly above the effective range of these extremely powerful weapons.

Smoke generators were positioned around some targets to help prevent visual bombing. Petrochemical plants were often protected by them because they were less likely to be damaged if the bombers had to rely on radar bombing.

*Left; The deadly German 88 mm Flak 36 anti-aircraft artillary guns were mounted on 'flak trains' to reinforce threatened areas targeted by Allied bombing.*

# BOMBS AWAY

The M-9 Norden bombsight juts out of the front of the B-17, behind the Plexiglas nose. It consists of two main parts: the sighthead, containing the optics, and the stabilizer, containing the gyroscope. The two parts are connected by the bombsight's connecting rod and clutch. Its precision telescopic rangefinder looks earthwards through a flat, undistorted panel in the Plexiglas.

*Right; The Fifteenth Air Force shows how bombs are dropped 'in train' with an appropriate intervalometer setting by 'Jocker', a B-17G of the 301st Bomb Group.*

The bombardier sits on his backless seat. He has stowed away the two-handled control wheel and trigger assembly with attached Sperry N-6A reflector gunsight he uses to control the chin turret. He concentrates his full attention on the bombsight, bending double over it as his eye looks through the optical eyepiece. His hands reach for the switches on the control panel.

The bombardier prepared the bombsight –including spinning up its stabilizing gyroscope –by the time the B-17 turned at the IP. The bombardier entered the wind, airspeed, and altitude calculations supplied by the navigator. A barometric altimeter provides the altitude information. The bombardier also sets the intervalometer, which determines how long the interval would be between bombs being released, to the pre-briefed figure.

Turning at the IP, the bombardier waits a few seconds until the B-17 is in straight and level flight towards the target.

'Bombardier to pilot, hold for level'. The pilot watches his instruments for a few seconds, making sure the B-17 is level and at its bombing altitude.

'Pilot to bombardier, level'.

The bombardier adjusts the bubbles in the spirit levels on the bombsight to make sure that it is level, and then uncages the stabilizing gyro. Now, even as the B-17 shakes, from turbulence or from flak bursts, the bombsight will remain stable. He switches on the bomb rack by moving the toggle switch, then moves it a further detent to 'open'.

'Bomb bay doors coming open'.

The bombardier hears the bomb bay doors open with a whirring grind. The drag of the open doors slows the B-17. The gunners in the back get a blast of icy cold air. The radio operator checks to see that both doors have come fully down. In the cockpit, the pilot gently retrims the B-17, so that it is stable with the doors open.

A three-minute straight and level bomb run was required for maximum accuracy when bombing visually. This proved very difficult in the teeth of German flak concentrations. The pilot sees the group ahead coming over the target and the churning black puffs of the flak. But the co-pilot is keeping the B-17 on course, as his attention is given to the final adjustments to the autopilot on the central console under the throttles, twisting input knobs to reflect the speed, altitude, and power settings of the bomb run.

'Bombardier to pilot, ready for bomb run'.

'Pilot to bombardier, it's your airplane'.

The pilot engages the Automatic Flight Control Equipment (AFCE). The bombardier will fly the plane through the autopilot as he adjusts the bombsight. It will fly to the spot in the sky where the mechanical ballistic computer inside the Norden bombsight's 'black box' has computed the moment of bomb release required to hit the target. The use of the autopilot on the bomb run prevents over-correction by the pilot to spoken instructions or violent evasive action. The pilot and co-pilot take their hands off the control wheels or let them rest on it, feeling the wheels move with small, metallic, tugs from the autopilot. AFCE could be easily overpowered and disengaged in an emergency. But when the pilots of lead ships do this, out of self-preservation, it disrupts the bombing of those following, for the Eighth Air Force in 1944 normally bombs on the leader, dropping their bombs when they see the lead ships drop.

Even as he flies the airplane, the bombardier has to keep it from destruction by flak. Every ten to 20 seconds, he twists in an evasive turn into the bombsight control's turn knob. If the pilot has set the autopilot accurately, this makes a coordinated turn, usually five degrees to keep accuracy, but it can be up to 15 degrees. This denies the flak a clear shot against a straight and level bomb run. The turn angles and directions are pre-planned so that the final turn, that straight over the target, can be made downwind.

The bombardier identifies the target, either by spotting the target markers dropped by the group or wing lead ship or by comparing it to the photographs at the briefing. Because of the limited field of view of the bomb sight, he must first look through the Plexiglas nose to make sure he can see the target before he uses the bombsight.

Looking through the eyepiece, the bomber sees the two electrically illuminated reticules, horizontal and vertical, the Norden's more sophisticated version of a cross-hair. He will use these and two indices at the side of his scope picture to aim and drop his bombs. The bombardier uses the computing capabilities of the Norden bombsight to compensate for the two factors that caused inaccuracy, drift (errors perpendicular to the bomber's flight path) and rate of change (errors along the bomber's flight path). The bombardier first compensates for drift, indicated by the target moving across the vertical reticule, by turning the bombsight's drift and turn knobs. This changes the B-17's direction of flight, via the AFCE, and makes the target appear to move down the bombsight's vertical reticule, and not drift off to either side. The bombardier has entered the drift angle into the bombsight's computer, calculated by the navigator with his E6B machine.

He begins tracking the target. He establishes the rate of change by how fast the target moves down the vertical reticule to the horizontal reticule. He compensates for rate by turning the rate knob, moving the horizontal reticule, to synchronize the bombsight. He would know he had achieved this when the target appeared stationary at the intersection of the horizontal and vertical reticules when looking through the bombsight's scope.

Finally, the target below and the bombsight synchronized, the bombardier looks through his eyepiece at the right side of the sight picture, where angle and rate indices moved to meet each other across his field of view. When they come together, the bombs drop automatically. The bombsight's crosshairs marks the spot where the bombs will impact, their forward travel from the bomber's speed computed from the type of bombs, altitude,

*Above; Targets, such as Nurnberg under this 487th Bomb Group B-17G, were often obscured by fires and impact smoke from preceding groups.*

*Left; Bombs sent for close salvo, B-17Gs of the 91st Bomb Group bomb 'on the leader'. The smoke trails are from air markers fired from the lead ships.*

and computed winds. The bombardier manually toggles the bomb release at the same time as a back-up.

'Bombs away' the bombardier calls over the intercom.

Depending on the intervelometer setting, it usually takes a few seconds for the bomb bay to empty. The bombardier watches through the bombsight. Olive drab bombs fall below the B-17, wobble a little, then gain stability as they accelerate under the influence of gravity. The bombardier keeps his eye on the bombsight, hoping to see where the bombs hit among the smoke and explosions from the preceding group. The pilot has already felt the bomber twitch and rise a little as each bomb dropped.

On the B-17s fitted with them, the radio operator operates the strike camera for photographs of how accurate the bombing has been and how much damage has been inflicted. He must also check the bomb bay for any hung-up bombs. Using the Morse key on the HF radio, the radio operators of the lead ships transmits the codewords that signify to England: 'primary bombed'.

*Below; A string of 500-pound bombs on their way to the target through the overcast after radar bombing from a B-17.*

# THE NORDEN BOMBSIGHT AND PRECISION DAYLIGHT BOMBING

The B-17's bombing tactics were based around the capabilities of the Norden bombsight. The Norden's gyro-stabilization and connection to the bomber's autopilot was cutting edge technology in the late 1930s. Its accuracy in pre-war tests provided the basis for 0the USAAF's confidence in strategic daylight bombing. Of course, these test were conducted with hand-picked crews, in New Mexico, with no one shooting at them. In wartime, hastily trained crews flying in northern Europe under massive flak fire could not achieve such accuracy.

Originally, every B-17 was to have used its Norden bombsight to bomb individually. However, the shortage of Norden bombsights in much of 1942-43 meant that often only formation lead ships and the deputy leads would have them. The Eighth Air Force in 1944-45, when using visual or radar bombing, would usually 'bomb on leader', and many bombers did not carry a bombardier, but rather a 'toggleer' to drop the bombs and operate the nose turret. The Fifteenth Air Force, however, continued to emphasize individual ship bombing.

While there were a number of attacks for which everything worked as in pre-war theory, in reality, the USAAF never achieved daylight precision bombing on a sustained basis. Half of its total bomb tonnage was dropped by radar, which was only effective against area targets. The tremendous size of the bomber offensive was required because it was necessary to put a large number of bombers over the target to place a few bombs on vital spots on the target

*Above; One of the most important transportation targets in Germany, the Aschaffenburg rail yards were paid a visit by Eighth Air force B-17s during 1944 with the resulting devastation.*

*Left; Smoke rising from air markers fired from the group lead ships are a signal for these 91st Bomb Group B-17Gs to begin bombing 'on the leader'.*

## BOMBING COURSE AND RANGE

The Norden gyro-stabilized bombsight was linked to the B-17's Honeywell auto-pilot through automatic flight control equipment. It would compute heading, drift, speed and height which were entered by the lead bombardier. On a bombing mission, each squadron, group and wing had a lead bombardier and lead ships were later equipped with H2X radars developed from the British H2S device which proved invaluable when bad weather over targets in Northern Europe threatened to abort many missions.

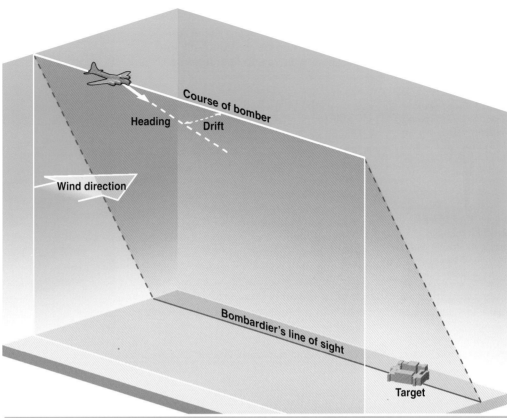

Course of bomber
Heading
Drift
Wind direction
Bombardier's line of sight
Target

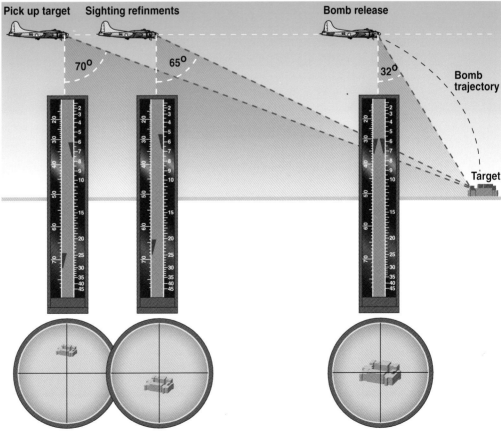

Pick up target    Sighting refinements                    Bomb release
70°              65°                        32°          Bomb trajectory
Target

# RETURN FLIGHT

'Pilot to bombardier, I've got it'.
The AFCE is disengaged. The bombardier spins down the gyros and turns off the bombsight, then swings his turret controls back into place. It's the pilot's airplane again and he has to take it home.

*Right; A 452nd Bomb Group B-17G streaming contrails with bomb bay doors agape just before dropping its warload of M47 incendiaries.*

*Below; After taking a direct hit from flak during its straight and level bomb run over the target, a doomed Eighth Air Force B-17 falls out of the formation in flames with one engine missing.*

As soon as the bomb bay door is closed, the pilot's first task is to re-trim the B-17 for level flight without its bombload. Now the bomber has an extra 10 or more mph of speed at the same power settings. The pilot calls out an intercom check of the crew, to see that all are still uninjured and have their oxygen working.

'Ball turret to pilot. Tight pattern, right on the target. Secondary explosions and fire'.

Without its bomb load, the B-17 now can turn or climb quicker when it changes course every ten to 20 seconds to evade flak. The B-17 joins in the formation's turn off the target, the time-to-turn after bombs away and the course both pre-briefed to keep the formation together.

The RP (Rally Point) is where formations re-assemble after coming off the target. It is normally located on a recognizable landmark away from flak concentrations, offset so that the lead group off the target must make a 45-90 degree turn, misleading the enemy. The altitude for the RP is often below bombing altitude, allowing the bombers to come off the target in a shallow dive, getting them away from the flak quicker and changing altitude to mislead enemy gunners.

In the group and wing lead ships, the command pilots in the right hand seats rely on the pilots that are sitting in their tail gun positions to survey the following bombers and their formation. They make a quick decision, assessing which B-17s are out of formation and whether they need time to catch up. Thus, even in the face of intense flak, the first groups off the target may have to slow down,

making S-turns, to allow those behind to join the formation. At the RP after the Regensburg raid of 16 August 1943, Brigadier General Curtis Le May, flying as command pilot in the Third Bomb Division (as it was then designated) lead ship, broke radio silence to upbraid the lead ship of the 100th Bomb Group for coming off the target in formation with only its two wingmen. The reply: this is the group. The other eighteen B-17s had all been knocked down, the formation getting tighter all the way to the target. So was born the legend of the 'Bloody Hundreth'.

The group combat box formations take up their place again in the combat wing formations and then the compact mass of the air division. In effect, they are repeating the morning's form-up over the buncher beacon, only now they do it under fire. From the RP, the formation sets its course for home.

*Above; The 5,000th B-17 delivered from Boeing's Seattle plant, '5 Grand' was autographed by the work force and covered with preservative shellac which added to its weight and increased drag. Despite this, it survived 78 combat missions over Germany.*

# SINGLE ENGINE FIGHTER ATTACKS

The German fighters' tactical instructions call for them to press home attacks even through flak, but bomber formations often find a respite from fighter attack after dropping the bombs. The Germans stand off out of range of the flak or are vectored against the bombers that have yet to drop their bombs. Because of this, the fighter escort may not fly close escort over the target, avoiding needless losses to flak, especially unaimed barrage fire. Against distant targets such as Berlin, the P-51 fighter groups that provided escort on the outward leg will now be released to strafe targets of opportunity, and the bombers will be met, coming off the targets, by fresh groups that have flown out from England to escort them home.

From the cockpit of the B-17 the pilot looks forward through the windshield. Dozens of contrails approach the formation from directly ahead. From that direction, they are not likely to be P-51s. Indeed, he can see the swirling intertwined contrails: dogfights with the fighter escort.

'Many bandits, twelve o'clock high. They're heading for the group ahead of us'. The pilot alerts the crew over the intercom.

Loose formations seem to attract the Luftwaffe. That is the same outfit that flew formation like Lancasters, left more ragged by the flak and formation changes over the target. Massed German fighter attacks could still be as deadly in 1944 as they had been in 1943, but most of the German fighters make a slashing attack, diving through a formation.

Looking at the group ahead, the pilot sees the B-17s weave and oscillate in evasive action. Tracers from the .50 calibers arc through the air. In the formation there are the gigantic black bursts of German 210 mm unguided rockets detonating. Seconds later, the attackers –FW 190s, scattered as single

*Left; The destruction of this Luftwaffe Bf 109G was recorded by the gun camera of a USAAF P-51 escort fighter in late 1944.*

## FIGHTER FORMATION

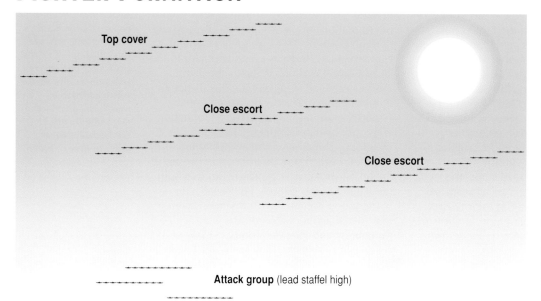

Top cover

Close escort

Close escort

Attack group (lead staffel high)

*Those German fighters carrying rockets or additional cannon proved vulnerable to USAAF escort fighters, so the Luftwaffe was forced to use standard fighter aircraft to provide top cover for the 'bomber destroyers'. This is the B-17 tail gunner's view of an incoming attack: three squadrons of German fighters escorting an 'attack staffel' that will soon open fire on the B-17 formation.*

ships and pairs –attack the formation from behind, and dive away, followed by the tracers of the tail gunners.

The B-17's pilot fixes his eye on one of the FW-190s for a moment, then sees it explode into flame as soon as it gets outside of the range of the B-17's tail guns. Like the German fighter pilot, he had not seen the P-51s diving from above. Now the Mustangs zoom climb to position themselves for another attack.

'There's a B-17 hit, 11 o'clock low'. The call over the intercom tells the pilot that the fighter attack has scored some hits. A B-17 from the group ahead is out of formation, trailing smoke from one wing. Unable to maintain speed and altitude despite having dropped its bombs, the damaged B-17 keeps to the same course of the formation, but the distance between it and the group behind decreases.

'The B-17 at 10 o'clock low's lost two engines.'

'It's on fire'. Another report over the intercom.

The pilot glances away from the horizon to the damaged B-17. Flames are now visible on the wing. He sees a small dark shape flash by its tail.

'They're bailing out. Watch for parachutes,' he alerts the crew over the intercom.

'There's two –no, three – out the bomb bay'. The B-17's bomb bay also serves as an emergency exit.

'There goes the tail gunner'. The tail gunner had his own escape hatch, just forward of his position.

'One out the crew door'. This is where the other gunners were to bail out from.

'Two out the nose hatch'. The bombardier and the navigator, rather than climb over the flight deck, could drop through the small hatch in the nose.

No-one else would escape that B-17. The stricken bomber is now just a lump of metal that does not belong at 25,000 feet. It starts an uncontrollable tight turn, a violent, uncontrollable spin. The 'g' forces –each turn is made at a force several times that of gravity –will pin the crewmen still inside. The B-17 will spin until it breaks apart in midair or augurs itself into the earth.

Parachutes blossom and drift through the smoke trail that marks the B-17's fall. During the Schweinfurt raids of 1943, there were so many it was said to look like an airborne invasion. The navigator records the time and position of the lost B-17 and the number of parachutes seen, to be reported at the debriefing

## REAR ATTACK

**Single or pairs of Fw 109 fighters attack any B-17 that drops behind its formation, making a diving rear attack with their 20 and 30mm cannon, breaking away before the tail gunner's .50 caliber machine guns get in range. German pilots learned to make a single, high-speed pass, not slowing down while within range of the bombers' machine guns.**

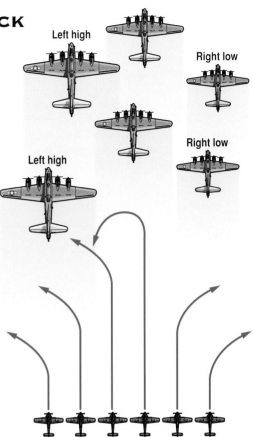

## FRONTAL ATTACK

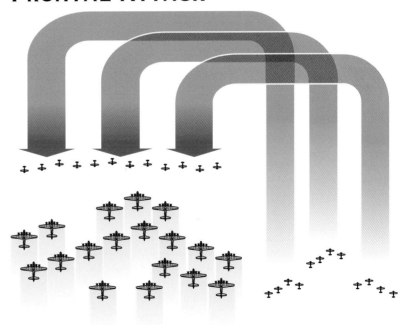

**In early 1943 the Germans learned to attack from head on where fewer defensive weapons could be brought to bear. However, the B-17G was fitted with a chin turret with twin .50 Brownings and by 1944, few pilots had the skill to hit a B-17 in the few seconds available at such high closing speeds.**

# TWIN-ENGINE FIGHTER ATTACKS

**More German fighters appear. Most do not make it through the fighter escorts. Others make slashing, diving attacks on the bombers. Between attacks, the crew glance at their oxygen control panels, looking for the blinker light that signaled a continuing flow. Icing, battle damage or malfunction would often cut off the oxygen. Crewmen may collapse before they could re-establish the flow. If this happened, another crewman would leave his station with a walk-around bottle and revive him.**

American fighters. The German fighters climb to attack. A Bf-110 and a Ju-88 turn in, climbing, dead astern of the B-17.

In 1943, the German twin engine fighters would stay back and shoot at the B-17s from long range, but now, slowing down to do this will attract the attentions of the P-51s. Instead, a mile behind the bombers, they have firewalled their throttles to get as much airspeed out of their heavily laden aircraft. They will overtake the B-17 formation as quick as they can. They close into range, using the bomber's contrails for concealment. They plan to fire a salvo of 210 mm rockets from under their wings and fire the 30 mm cannon under their fuselage. If they can damage a B-17 enough to make it drop out of formation, they can finish it off with their nose-mounted 20 mm cannon.

'Fighters. Here they come. Six o' clock low, One Me-110. Five o'clock high, one Ju-88.' The flight engineers rotate their turrets to the rear to engage the Ju-88. The B-17's two wingmen also open fire, as do the gunners in other elements. The tail gunner sees them. He and the ball turret gunner open fire at the Bf-110.

The ball turret gunner is hunched between the breeches of his two machine-guns, with the optical display of the K-4 reflector gunsight in front of his face. He pulls lead on the Bf-110, adjusting the gunsight reticules with a lever under his left foot. He uses two

*Above; Streaming a contrail, the Luftwaffe Fw 190 in the top left positions itself for a 'pursuit curve' attack on the two B-17 in the foreground.*

*Right; 'Chopsticks', a pathfinder B-17G with H2X radar in the nose, goes down in flames over Berlin on March 6, 1944. Lead ship of the entire 3rd Air Division formation, the wing's commander was lost in this 482nd Bomb Group Fort.*

'B-17 falling behind the formation'.

It loses altitude and speed, falling below and behind the formation but still keeping the course for home. The B-17's tail gunner reports this over the intercom –the navigator hastily jots it down in pencil in his log for later incorporation into the report.

'He's firing green flares'.

The ball turret gunner has also watched the straggler fall behind. Green flares are the general SOS signal to the fighter escort: 'Save me, I am under attack'. In a few seconds the threat to the straggler comes a lot closer to home. The ball turret is the first to see them.

'Bandits, seven o'clock low, bunch of twin-engine and single engines both'. It is a reduced strength staffel-sized unit of Ju-88Cs and Bf-110s, carrying rockets and extra cannons. Their close escort of Bf-109s will try to protect the twin-engine fighters from the P-51s. Caught on their own, these twin-engine aircraft would stand no chance against

## B17 v ME110: REAR ATTACK 1

The outdated twin-engine Me 110 had been outclassed in the Battle of Britain in 1940 and would only attack B-17 formations if the bombers were unescorted. However, the hitting power of its 30mm MK 108 cannon could inflict terminal damage on a heavily laden Fortress from a 1,000 yards.

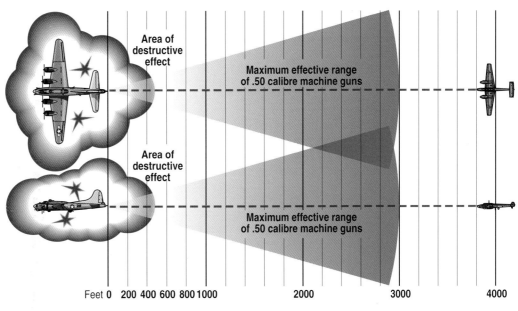

Area of destructive effect

Maximum effective range of .50 calibre machine guns

Area of destructive effect

Maximum effective range of .50 calibre machine guns

Feet 0  200 400 600 800 1000  2000  3000  4000

post handles projecting rearward above the sight to rotate and depress the turret. When he has the fighter in his sights, he depresses the red firing buttons at the end of each handle.

The B-17's Cheyenne tail gun position (named after the modification depot where it was first installed) gives the tail gunner greater visibility through bullet proof glass and a correspondingly greater field of fire against this attack. He uses the spade grip to move and fire the twin machine-guns remotely rather than manhandling them. A Sperry N-8 reflector gunsight replaced the ring-and-bead of earlier B-17 tail guns, projecting the familiar red reticule with a red center dot. While the German's heavy armament outranges the .50 calibers, in a tail attack the defending gunners have the benefit that their projectiles are closing quickly with the enemy aircraft heading towards them, while the attacker's projectiles must first 'overtake' the target. The same weapon has a more effective backwards than forwards reach.

At 2,000 yards (1828 m), the twin-engine fighters fire their 210 mm rockets. These burst in the formation with large black puffs, like flak. Closing to 1,200 yards (1096 m), the Germans open fire with their 30 mm cannon. These are massive shells, each with its own tracer shoe, but slow firing. The tail gunner in the B-17 feels as if he can see every shell, all aimed at him. Firing, the Germans close in to 800 yards (731 m) then, seeing the return .50 caliber fire becoming more accurate, the Bf-

110 slow-rolls and breaks away to the left in a steep dive, while the Ju-88 breaks away to the right, wing-up. As they turn out of range of the B-17, the tail gunner sees a flight of four P-51s appear in a diving turn, splitting to attack the twin-engine fighters before they can rejoin.

## B17 v ME110: REAR ATTACK 2

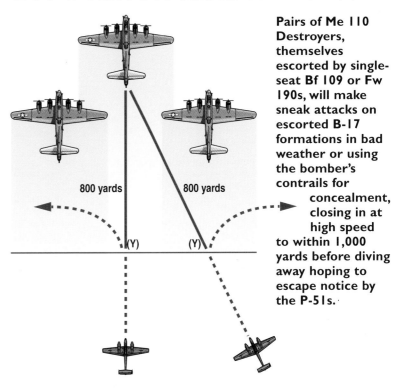

800 yards    800 yards

(Y)    (Y)

Pairs of Me 110 Destroyers, themselves escorted by single-seat Bf 109 or Fw 190s, will make sneak attacks on escorted B-17 formations in bad weather or using the bomber's contrails for concealment, closing in at high speed to within 1,000 yards before diving away hoping to escape notice by the P-51s.

# ENGINE FIRE

**The pilot feels the B-17 shake. Instinctively, his head swivels around. Smoke streams out of the inboard engine from under the cowl flaps.**

'Fire in number two engine'. The procedures, in yet another checklist, are long since committed to memory.

The smoke is the light gray of burning gasoline rather than the dark black of an oil fire. The pilot's right hand pushes the throttle of the burning engine forward, running up the engine in an attempt to blow out the fire. Six or seven very long seconds pass, but all this does is make the flames larger.

'Close the cowl flaps on number two engine'.

The co-pilot closes the cowl flaps. The pilot closes the fuel selector valve to number two engine, hoping to cut off the fuel and so put out the fire. He places the propeller pitch control in 'high rpm' which quickly scavenges the fuel line and engine of gasoline.

A B-17 losing an engine swings towards the lost engine. In the midst of these emergency procedures, the pilot and co-pilot must keep the B-17 back to an even keel. The pilot keeps up the left wing.

'Select fire extinguisher, number two engine'.

'Fire extinguisher, number two'. The co-pilot repeats the command, to make sure that he's heard it correctly and that the pilot has given the right command. More than once, a perfectly good engine has been extinguished by mistake. The co-pilot clicks the fire extinguisher selector valve to the number two position. The engine's still burning.

'Pull first charge'. The co-pilot pulls on the red fire extinguisher handle. Even with the closed cowl flaps, the carbon dioxide gas from the extinguisher can be seen as some escapes into the slipstream.

'Pull second charge'. That seems to do it. No more flames. The pilot checks the instruments. Fuel pressure has dropped to zero.

'Stop number two engine'. The co-pilot pulls back the mixture control of number two engine to the detent labeled 'engine off' and switches off the booster pump. The propeller still turns. The engine is effectively dead, but its windmilling propeller is a source of drag that can force the B-17 out of formation. To stop the propeller windmilling, its blades need to be turned edge-on to the airflow, 'feathering' them.

*Right; A moment of extreme danger. A B-17F straggler loses altitude over enemy territory with smoke streaming from its flak-damaged inboard engine.*

'Feather two'.

'Feather two'. The co-pilot again repeats the command and then presses the feathering switches.

Slowly, the propeller pitch changes and the propeller stops. The pilot pulls back the throttle to number two engine, followed by the turbo-supercharger control and the mixture control, and cuts the generator and the voltage regulator, so that there will be no electricity that could re-ignite the fire. Failure of propellers to feather –due to the fire damaging the mechanism or lack of oil –contributed to the loss of many B-17s. Early production B-17Gs were particularly vulnerable due to deletion of an engine standpipe that held reserve oil.

In the few seconds it took to fight the fire,

the B-17 lurched out of formation. Now, increasing power on the three remaining engines, it is able to climb back, ahead of its two wingmen. With its bombload gone and without the drag of the windmilling propeller, the B-17 will be able to keep formation on three engines by increasing power.

The pilot compensates with higher power settings on the three good engines, while maintaining directional control with the rudder. This will increase the fuel consumption of the remaining engines. As soon as the fighter attacks cease, the flight engineer will transfer fuel from number two to the operable engines. He also keeps a close eye on the gauges of the three remaining engines. With an engine out, they must be run at higher rpms and boost than

usual, increasing the chance of an engine failure. Three-engine flight is not difficult for an unloaded B-17; two engines out is always an emergency.

It gets very cold inside the B-17 without the number two engine: this had been supplying hot air through the fuselage, but now sends cold air from the airflow. The loss of number two engine has knocked out the B-17's highly effective glycol heating system. Fortunately, the flight instruments that depended on the vacuum pump on number two engine can be cross-selected to feed off the vacuum pump on number three engine. However, this means that this pump will not be available for operating the black de-icing boots on the leading edge of the wings if required on the return to base.

# HOMEWARD LEG

Once the returning formation had left German airspace, the worst of the flak and fighters was past. Yet even in 1944 the Germans could still attack returning bombers, even intercepting them over their bases in England, so relaxing vigilance was not a good idea. However, the B-17's pilot breaks radio silence to ask a wingman to examine the damage on number two engine.

Not all the stragglers are able to maintain altitude all the way home. Over the North Sea, escort fighters will call RAF air-sea rescue for those bomber crews that are forced to ditch. A B-17 could float for five minutes or more, enough time to deploy the big orange life rafts.

Aboard the B-17, the radio operator turns the IFF transponder back on to identify it as friendly to radars along the English coast. He tunes the ADF back in to friendly radio beacons and starts providing fixes to the navigator.

Stragglers following the formation are often intercepted by the RAF, especially if their IFF is damaged or malfunctioning. They may be led to one of the master emergency fields, Manston or Bentwaters, with wide runways and rescue equipment on stand-by. Other aircraft out of formation can be tracked on radar and directed home by navigational directions over the voice radio.

Once the bombers cross the English coast, there is a de-assembly of the formations: a mirror image of the complex formation assembly of the morning. First, the air divisions split apart, then the combat wings, over the buncher beacons at the coast. The combat wings then fly to the splasher

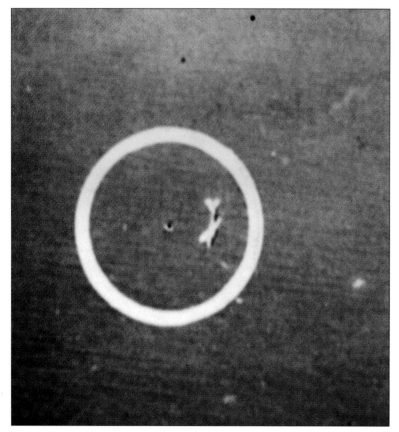

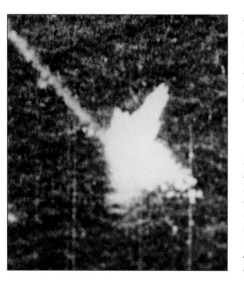

*Above and Left: Damaged over Germany, a B-17F goes out of control and plummets into the North Sea. Observers in other bombers will report the location in the hope that any survivors can be rescued.*

*Right; A save for the RAF. A lifeboat is dropped from a Hudson of RAF Coastal Command to a ditched B-17 in the North Sea. In one mission to Stuttgart on September 6, 1943, twelve B-17s ditched and 118 crewmen were rescued by the RAF.*

*Left; USAAF B-17Fs seen through the waist window of the element lead as they head for home after a bombing mission over Germany in 1943.*

*Below; Having made it all the way back to England and within sight of its base, this B-17 crash lands in an East Anglian field.*

beacons, where the combat groups shake themselves out so that each Bomb Group's planes are, in heading for their own bases, identified by nearby buncher beacons. The lead navigators use these beacons and the ADF, plus pilotage and dead reckoning, to make sure their formations return to the right base. Today, the morning overcast has burnt off, so there is no need for a letdown on instruments.

*Left; The welcome sight of England's patchwork quilt of fields greets the crew of this 381st Bomb Group B-17G as it lets down to its base in East Anglia.*

*Right; B-17G 'Mary Kay' of 91st Bomb Group, known as the 'Ragged Irregulars' in the foreground was shot down by German fighters during a raid on Oberpfaffendorff on March 18, 1944.*

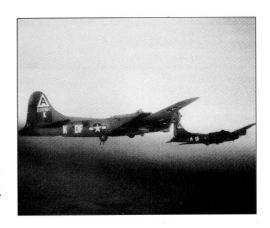

# RETURNING TO BASE

**Gradually losing altitude, the group formation flies from the splasher beacon to the base. The voice VHF radios are tuned to the base's approach frequency, which provides the returning formation with the day's brevity codes informing them of the active runway they are to land on, the current direction and speed of the winds, and the air pressure (to properly set the barometric altimeter).**

On board the B-17, there is a pre-landing checklist to do. The ball gunner hauls himself out of his cramped turret, which is now locked in place under the airplane. The crew takes the same stations they had for take-off, the gunners appraising the damaged engine and the feathered number two propeller through the radio room windows.

With the formation now down to 1,500 feet (457 m) altitude, the base is in sight ahead and to the left. Two-star red flares are fired from one of the B-17s in the formation: the

signal for wounded aboard. The pilot hears an unfamiliar voice over the VHF command radio identify this B-17 to the tower by the last three digits of its serial number and requests a straight-in approach. It's granted. The pilot sees this B-17 descend out of the formation, flying towards a point where, 'leading' the turn so it rolls out aligned with the main runway, a 90 degree turn puts it on a final approach.

While the ship with wounded aboard makes its straight-in approach, the formation passes upwind over the field at 1,500 feet (457 m). The sound of massed engines is audible on the base. Everyone on the ground stops what they are doing and counts the returning B-17s. Not only ground crew, but command and staff, administrative and technical personnel and flight crews that were not on the mission come outside watch the returning B-17s. More ominously, the crash trucks, fire engines and the ambulances wait, engines turning over. Firemen don protective suits. The flight surgeon checks his instruments.

As the B-17s come over the runway, the squadrons go into trail formation. Each three plane 'vee' is now following each other. Precision in landing embodies the fundamental ethos of military aviation. With large numbers of aircraft, at slow speed, in close proximity to each other and the ground, the object is getting them all down in the shortest possible time without additional hazard. There is also the pride in flying a tight formation overhead the field.

At the upwind end of the runway, the three B-17s of the lead element begin a 90 degree descending left turn into the crosswind leg of

*Above; The command staff of an Eighth Air force bomber base in England, on the roof of the control tower straining to get their first sight of the returning B-17s.*

*Right; Having been alerted to damaged aircraft and wounded air crews, the airfield crash crews, ambulance and fire truck stand by as the first of the bombers return.*

the traffic pattern, at 1,000 feet (304 m). The three ships of the lead element, in turn, lower their landing gears and go into trail formation, the two wingmen rolling out of the turn behind their leader. They will extend their spacing as they fly the pattern –crosswind, a left turn to the downwind leg, a left turn to the base leg, and finally a left turn to final approach, lined up with the runway –so that they will keep proper spacing on final approach: 20-seconds to a minute depending on conditions.

The precision flying in the pattern is helped by the B-17's stable slow flight characteristics. There is little danger of a stall from these unloaded bombers. They are at 150 mph entering the crosswind leg and without bombs or much fuel, the B-17 stalls with flap and gear down at about 80 mph. It does not drop a wing, but ham-handed recoveries could lead to secondary stalls.

The pilot now must go over more checklist items. He orders the co-pilot to open the carburetor air filters. With his right hand he moves the supercharger controls to full 'on' and the propeller to 'locked low pitch'. Approaching the point to turn into the pattern, with the speed below the 147 mph maximum for gears or flap, the pilot orders 'Gear down'. The co-pilot puts the landing gear switch in the 'down' position. But the electrical whirr and clunk of landing gear extension sounds and feels different. Even as he hears the co-pilot report 'right gear down' and the flight engineer report 'tailwheel down', the pilot sees that the left main landing gear has not come down.

The pilot first orders the co-pilot: 'Add power'. He announces over the VHF voice radio that the B-17 will not be entering the landing pattern due to a stuck landing gear. The wingmen, seeing the one gear trailing, continue their turn without the element leader, which continues upwind.

'Gear up'.

Power, pitch, and turbosuperchargers adjusted, the B-17 climbs slightly, heads for a nearby landmark which has been designated as a holding point for landing. The pilot puts the B-17 into a gentle turn. Throttling back, he again orders: 'Gear down'.

Again, the left main gear stays firmly in the wing.

'Lower left gear manually'. The pilot orders over the intercom, turning off the electric landing gear switch.

In the radio room, the radio operator unstraps himself and removes the large steel, olive-drab handcrank stowed on the rear

bulkhead of the radio compartment. He sidles along the catwalk through the bomb bay, sticking his head into the flight deck and gesturing to the crank. The pilot gives him a thumbs up. This is the radio's operator signal to insert the crank into its connection in the bomb bay, on the left side of the B-17, and starts cranking the main gear down.

The gear finally down –evidenced by the green indicator lights in the cockpit and visual inspection –and locked, the next step is to check hydraulic pressure. It is normal (800 pounds) which suggests that the hydraulic lines have not been damaged by the engine fire. The toe brakes are also tested and seem to be working. The pre-landing checklist is repeated again, power adjusted, the airplane trimmed for gear-down flight, the pilot calls the tower that the B-17 is ready to descend to pattern altitude re-enter the traffic pattern. The tower clears him to land.

*Top; As the returning formation comes overhead the airfield, these 92nd Bomb Group bombers begin to peel off and join the traffic pattern.*

*Above; 'Wagtail II', a 31st Bomb Group B-17F flies over East Anglia at the end of a mission in the summer of 1943.*

# TRAFFIC PATTERN AND LANDING

**Ahead, over the field, the tail-end Charlie, the last B-17 in the formation, did not land but instead, once the runway was clear of the preceding airplane, made a high-speed low-altitude pass down the runway centerline before climbing up and turning to join the pattern for landing. Without the weight of bombs or fuel, the stable B-17 is a pleasure to fly at 30 feet (9 m) and 200 mph. This is an official 'buzz job' by a crew that had just completed the last mission of its tour: 25 missions for most of the bomber offensive, 30, then 35 from 1944.**

*Above: An engine out, this 385th Bomb Group B-17F is a little high over the numbers but otherwise fine on final approach.*

The tower clears the B-17 to enter the downwind leg of the pattern in a right turn, away from the dead engine. The B-17 flies downwind, parallel to the runway, at pattern altitude: 1,000 feet (304 m) and 140 mph. The turbosuperchargers provide 30, then decreasing to about 25 inches of manifold pressure when all four engines are turning. With one engine dead, the pilot has to keep up boost and rpms on the three remaining engines, cowl flaps now open and locked for cylinder head cooling. The next turn –turning base leg –is to the left, into the dead engine and is more difficult. The trim tabs are neutral and pilot compensates with power on number one engine and uses the rudder to keep the turn coordinated, the ball centered in the turn and bank indicator, and not 'fall off' towards the dead engine.

As soon as the B-17 has rolled out of its turn onto the base leg of the traffic pattern, the pilot orders: 'Airspeed, 135; one third flaps'.

While the pilot keeps his eye on the numbers designating the runway, the spot he is aiming to touch down, the co-pilot gently pulls back the throttles, still keeping number one ahead, and watches the airspeed

indicator. As it drops below 137 mph indicated, he clicks the wing flap switch on his side of the throttle console to the one-third position.

The flaps come down with an electric whirr and the airplane slows down. Thanks to the B-17's stability there is still no need to re-trim. There is another left turn coming up, onto final approach, only this time the B-17 is slower and, with its partially lowered flaps, has both more lift and more drag. Again, he compensates for the dead engine and leads the turn, so that he rolls out pointing straight at the runway's identifying numbers, one thousand feet below.

It all happens very fast on final approach. 'Airspeed, 120. Propellers to high RPM. Full flaps'.

The co-pilot responds to the orders. The throttles come back. The turbo-supercharger's boost goes down to 20 inches of pressure. The flap switch goes to the full down position, as they whirr and lock under the lower wings. The B-17 loses altitude rapidly. It's a good approach. The numbers painted on the runway stay in about the same position viewed through the windshield.

As the B-17 passes 300 feet (91 m) altitude, an unexpected crosswind gusts from the right. The B-17, as with any large tailwheel airplane, has problems landing in strong crosswinds, especially as the large fin and rudder lead to weather-vaning. The pilot compensates by dropping the right wing and crabbing into the wind, keeping pressure on the left rudder pedal.

'A touch more power'.

The pilot wants to keep the B-17 at 120 mph despite these maneuvers and the unexpected crosswind. Its stability means that it is slow to react and accelerate, but a burst of power helps keep it from a too-fast sink rate as it loses altitude. As a result, as the B-17 comes over the numbers, but high from the additional power. Unloaded B-17s want to fly and have a tendency to 'float' on landing. The feathered propeller compounds this effect. The co-pilot pulls back on the throttle. The pilot gently brings the nose forwards and lets go of the pressure on the rudder and raises the right wing a little.

The right main wheel touches down first, followed by the left a second later, raising puffs of smoke and a loud erk-erk sound from the tires. Like much else in the B-17's design, its landing gear is early 1930s technology, but

Above; Touchdown, 'Piccadilly Commando' of the 91st Bomb Group returns home to RAF Bassingbourn after a mission.

Above; A 'buzz job' at RAF Bassingbourn by the crew of a tour-completed B-17F of the 91st Bomb Group which suffered the heaviest losses of any Eighth Air force Group.

Below; The crew of this 305th Bomb Group B-17F brings their Fort in for an immaculate three point touchdown

Above; A B-17G of the 91st Bomb Group on final approach watched by the flight control van.

Above; The Flight Control van by the active runway will give a red flare to any airplane that does not have its gear down and locked.

strongly-built. The pilot gently pressures the rudder to keep the rolling B-17 aligned with the runway centerline until the tail wheel lowers and then drops. The flight engineer is standing by the hand-pump, but the hydraulic pressure comes through as the pilot and co-pilot gently start to tap the toe brakes as the B-17 slows. The B-17 comes to a stop near the end of the runway. It immediately turns to taxi off the runway, along the perimeter taxiway.

Left; Any landing you can walk away from is a good one even though this early B-17F is destined for cannibalization after breaking its back.

# BACK TO THE HARDSTAND

**The B-17 is easier to maneuver on the ground without the weight of the bombload and fuel. There is also no need for the B-17s to stay close together on the ground. There are also fewer coming back.**

*Below; The B-17 was highly survivable in belly landings, as long as the ball turret was jettisoned, in part because of the protruding main wheels. After substantial repairs, this 398th Bomb Group B-17G was transferred to the 91st Bomb Group.*

Approaching the hardstand, the crew chief is positioned in front to guide the B-17 in to park. The ground crew has 'sweated out' the mission at the hardstand and have strained to catch sight of 'their' B-17's return. Guided by the crew chief, the B-17 turns towards the hardstand and slowly rolls forward. Then, following directions and adding a little power to the outboard engine, the pilot and co-pilot turn the B-17 through 180 degrees with the inside wheel rolling (pivoting may blow the tire) until it is where is started the mission, nose pointing towards the taxiway.

The crew chief gives the 'cut' sign. On the flight deck, the pilot and co-pilot do their shut-down checklist. As the propellers spin down to a halt, ground crewmen chock the wheels.

The B-17's crew grabs equipment, removes outer flight clothing, and exits. Inspection of the damage is the first item, with flight and ground crew alike looking at the number two engine. There is not the large hole of a large-caliber direct hit. Apparently, a fragment severed one of the fuel lines in the engine, spraying the hot turbo-supercharger with 100-octane fuel. A few new flak holes are also noted for repair. The damage is repairable on base, probably at the hardstand, or else the B-17 will be taxiing over to the technical site for a new engine and repairs to the wing.

Before leaving the site, the gunners, assisted by the armorers will dismount and later clean, and store the machine-guns. The bombardier dismounts the Norden bombsight and secures it in its carrying case. A truck arrives to carry away photographs from the strike camera. The pilot updates the Form 1A and hands it to the crew chief.

# MISSION'S END

A truck appears at the hardstand to take the crew, first, to hand in bombsight and flight equipment, return their escape packs and pick up personal items. They then go for debriefing. This is conducted by the group intelligence officer and his staff. Navigators refer to their logs, which will later be written up and turned in.

Many of the crews are loud and animated, telling what they saw by using their hands in the universal sign-language of pilots. Many, their ears still ringing from the noise of the engines and the machineguns, require the debriefers to yell their questions; hearing loss was as common among B-17 crews as Air Medals. Some sit quietly, exhausted and expressionless, or politely answer the questions of the debriefers. Red Cross girls provide doughnuts and coffee and the mess hall sends over sandwiches. The flight surgeon may stand by to examine minor wounds or, often, provide a medicinal drink, appreciated by those still feeling the high-altitude cold.

Bombing accuracy and its component factors: altitude, position in the formation, cloud cover, is the primary interest at the

Above; Air crews are immediately debriefed by their pre-assigned debriefers who want to go throught the mission in great detail.

Left; The relief of being 'back home' is obvious on the faces of the young Eighth Air Force veterans as they carried from their B-17 by the groundcrew.

*Left; After each mission, the gunners have to remove and clean the B-17's .50 caliber machine guns before they are handed over to the armorers.*

*Above; The Luftwaffe airfield at Bad Albing showing the damage it received after a visit by Eighth Air Force bombers in 1944.*

debrief. The debrief needs to establish the damage done to the target and how accurate the bombing has been. These are vital in determining whether the target needs to be hit again. The bombing accuracy figures are important to determine expected future accuracy and identify needed improvements. The photographs from those B-17s fitted with strike cameras will be key in answering these questions.

The crew are also asked about the flak, its strength and location. The debrief also goes through the fighter attack, reviewing enemy numbers and tactics. These will be sent in an immediate message to wing, air division, and Pinetree, which will be used to plan subsequent missions, possibly as early as the next day. More elaborate reports will follow after the strike photographs are processed. Before the end of the day, once the smoke has

*Left; Mission's end. An Eighth Air Force B-17 Fortress makes a final sunset approach to its English base.*

*Right; After a shower and brief nap, a B-17's group NCOs - air and ground crew - gather around a piano together off duty until the next mission.*

*Above; A defiant German swastika is draped over the rubble of a devastated suburb of Berlin in 1945 following a daylight raid by USAAF Flying Fortresses.*

*Right; The view of Berlin being pounded by Eighth Air force B-17 bombers of the 95th Bomb Group, some of the 580 American bombers over the German capital on March 8, 1944.*

died down, high-altitude reconnaissance aircraft will fly over the target to get the final word on the strikes' effectiveness. The USAAF did not make the mistake of equating the scope of its efforts with the effectiveness of its results. The events seen by the crews on the mission are also recorded, especially the loss

of friendly aircraft. The circumstances and the number of parachutes spotted are entered in the Missing Air Crew Reports for each one lost.

Sometimes, crews would be put on alert for the next day's mission as soon as they completed the debrief, but except during maximum efforts, the same crews are unable to sustain such an operational tempo for more than a few days. Next day may be devoted to repairing airplanes and training. In this case, the crew can relax at the on-base clubs, a local pub or nearby town, or, go back to quarters and fall asleep. Some must secure the personal effects of friends who did not return and whose living quarters will be needed, immediately, by their replacements. The replacements may fly in later the same day, often in shiny new silver-tail B-17s that will have to receive the group's distinctive markings.

# SUMMARY

**The USAAF's contribution to the strategic bomber offensive was a massive undertaking in every sense: 365,000 sorties flown and one million tons of bombs dropped at the cost of 6,700 bombers lost in combat, and 62,000 men killed or captured. The cost was also tremendous in material terms. The USAAF absorbed about a quarter of the total US resources expended in the Second World War, and strategic bombing absorbed some 40 percent of that.**

*Above; A different load is dropped. A 390th Bomb Group B-17G drops food over the Netherlands in April 1945. The ball turret guns droop down, unmanned.*

What this and all the other sorties of the bomber offensive meant to the ultimate victory has been argued by historians for years. It is impossible to calculate precisely the effects of the bomber offensive. But the evidence is strong. Most German flak batteries and fighter squadrons were defending the Reich, not on the battlefronts. By 1944, damage to Germany's synthetic fuel industry meant that continued high production in other industries could not yield increased combat effectiveness. Panzer divisions stalled by the side of the road for lack of fuel. Fighter planes hid from the P-51s

in camouflaged dispersals. These were undeniable achievements of the bomber offensive. It was an indispensable part of the Allied war effort.

The type of air combat exemplified by this sortie, and those of RAF Bomber Command, effectively started in 1941-42 and ended in 1945. There have been a few reprises: the US Air Force (successor to the AAF) use of B-29s over Korea in 1950-53 and B-52s over Hanoi in 1972. But after 1945 heavy bombers were not committed over enemy territory in sustained strategic bombing campaigns directly against the enemy's will and means to resist rather than his forces in the field.

After Hiroshima and Nagasaki, the strategic bomber's mission became largely that of nuclear deterrence, rather than winning wars. Because one bomber could now do the damage of a thousand, there was no longer a need for massed bombers or their formation. The atom bomber would fly alone, operating either above –especially before the surface to air missile became widespread –or, later, below the defenses' radar coverage. Bombers like the B-17 were also no longer the only way to carry large quantities of conventional bombs long distances. The future was the P-38 'strategic fighter-bombers' used over Ploesti in 1944. They did not have to defend themselves with multiple turrets and gunners: the bombs could be delivered by a smaller airplane. Because they were smaller and more maneuverable, they could dive-bomb or attack from low altitude and deliver the bombs more accurately than from high altitude.

Already, in 1945, there were single-engine, single-seat tactical piston engine aircraft such as the US Navy's XBT2D-1 with massive 2,800 hp engines that allowed them to carry a bombload similar to a B-17. Once jet engines became more fuel-efficient in the 1950s, the widespread introduction of air refueling allowed these aircraft range comparable to the strategic bombers of the Second World War. When conventional munitions needed to be delivered by air, it was more effective to have tactical aircraft do it, especially with the rise of smart munitions starting in the 1970s.

This type of mission has vanished along with the B-17s that flew them. But the ideas that produced both the B-17 and the Eighth Air Force are still alive and evolving. The US Air Force, in the wake of the Gulf War of 1991, is reassessing anew its legacy of conventional precision bombing.

*Above; The 305th Bomb Group lay down a tight pattern of bombs on the Arado works at Ankelm where Fw 190s are built, on August 4, 1944.*

*Left; After the end of the war in Europe, US troops examine the heavy damage caused by Eighth Air Force B-17 bombers in the Spring of 1945 to this collapsed hangar at an airfield at Leipzig.*

# ACKNOWLEDGEMENTS

My thanks to The Experimental Aircraft Association, who allowed me to fly the left hand seat of their superbly restored B-17G, the 'Aluminum Overcast'. Making S-turns across Interstate 81 down the Shenandoah Valley introduced me to the responsiveness and stability of the B-17. And to my father, himself a former Eighth Air Force navigator, who took me to go inside a flyable B-17 at New York's Marine Air Terminal back in 1962. I recall another visitor –he seemed old –sitting in the radio operator's seat, intently and silently communing with the airplane and watching the ghosts of men and airplanes from twenty years before. That is why the B-17 will always be more than aluminum and avgas.